THE
ENCYCLOPEDIA
OF
JOINTMAKING

THE
ENCYCLOPEDIA
OF
JOINTMAKING

TERRIE NOLL

BETTERWAY BOOKS

A QUARTO BOOK

Copyright © 1997
Quarto Inc.

First Published in the U.S.A. by
Betterway Books, an imprint of
F & W Publications, Inc.
1507 Dana Avenue
Cincinnati, Ohio 45207
(800) 289 0963

ISBN 1-55870-449-3

This book was designed and produced
by Quarto Publishing plc
The Old Brewery
6 Blundell Street
London N7 9BH

Senior Editor Kate Kirby
Senior Art Editor Toni Toma
Designer Glyn Bridgewater
Prop Buyer Miriam Hyman
Picture Manager Giulia Hetherington
Photographer Paul Forrester
Illustrators Ed Roberts, Lawrie
Taylor, Kevin Maddison, Terry Hadler,
George Fryer
Editorial Director Mark Dartford
Art Director Moira Clinch

Typeset in Great Britain by
CST, Eastbourne
Manufactured in Singapore by
Universal Graphics Pte Ltd
Printed in China by
Leefung-Asco Printers Ltd

Contents

CHAPTER FIVE
Mortise and Tenon 67

CHAPTER SIX
Miters and Bevels 89

CHAPTER SEVEN
Dovetails 103

CHAPTER EIGHT
Dowels and Biscuits 117

CHAPTER NINE
Fasteners, Hardware, and Knockdown Joints 129

Foreword

Because the entire subject of woodworking would not fit between the covers of this book, the best resources for the proper, safe operation of your tools are the manuals that came with them, or other publications that specifically address tool usage and maintenance. The same is true for in-depth information about the characteristics of specific woods as they apply to woodworking. What has been packed into these covers is a very big slice of the woodworking pie—the subject of joinery.

I am a builder, so I had to start this book with two foundation chapters about basic things: the contrariness of wood and what to do about it, how wood parts form relationships, the vocabulary of elements for composing a joint, and what makes joints last. Mixed into these first chapters is a little consciousness raising about joinery-specific pitfalls that may present themselves in the form of inaccuracy and the dreaded operator error. A few friends for life make your acquaintance there, too, like the triangle marking system and layout story poles, which have been helping for centuries to keep parts confusion and measuring mistakes at bay. Armed and anchored by this joinery knowledge, the reader is safe to proceed into the subsequent practical chapters on specific joint families.

If you are a fledgling woodworker, you may be eager to start sawing and chiseling joints and skip ahead of the beginning. I always was. But when you recognize that the time has come to refine your technique, a few quiet moments with the theories and tricks in the early chapters are convincing evidence that in woodworking brightness should always precede brawn.

The body of chapters is graded from simpler to more complex

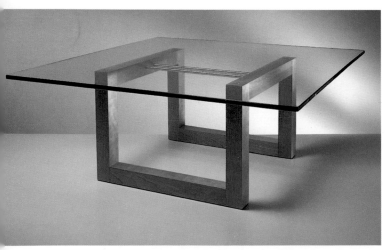

Make leg assemblies wth blind mortise and tenon, Chapter 5.

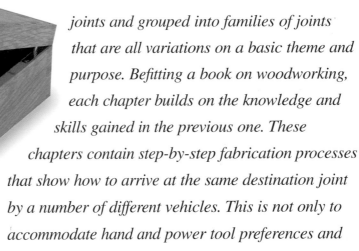

Chapter 7 shows easy precision dovetails like these.

joints and grouped into families of joints that are all variations on a basic theme and purpose. Befitting a book on woodworking, each chapter builds on the knowledge and skills gained in the previous one. These chapters contain step-by-step fabrication processes that show how to arrive at the same destination joint by a number of different vehicles. This is not only to accommodate hand and power tool preferences and budgets, but also to prevent tunnel vision from obscuring the roads to Rome. Paraphrasing the adage about all roads leading there, a woodworker should know the many avenues to a completed joint and pick the one which travels best for him or her. The chapters on joint families also serve as references for finding or sparking that elusive joint design, or to refresh some basic procedures for making it. To use the scientific search method, the index is the place to go. For the serendipitous, just thumb through and let fate take you where it will. The last chapter even includes a survey of hardware for making joints without any joinery at all.

There are always readers who like the end of the book first, and in that location is a glossary of terms and definitions that represent a good bit of information—a distilled version of this book. The glossary can teach and hopefully clarify the lingo that is native to woodworking country. The process of working wood is the mother of invention. I'd be surprised if readers didn't find a hundred and one ways to improve on the basic methods and rudimentary jigs included here, plus design new joint variations of their own. That's part of the divine plan for every creative woodworker and anyone who likes to shop through tool catalogs. I hope you'll consider this book a good start.

Edge laps from Chapter 4 create a display box.

CHAPTER ONE

AIDS TO ACCURACY AND ORDER

Woodworking takes rough lumber through a process of refinement, dividing and shaping it into mated parts that assemble to create a new form. Starting with the raw material and moving through to clamping, this chapter shows how to mark the steps, organize parts, clamp and check for accuracy, plus select and check the layout tools themselves.

Dressing Rough Lumber

After logs are sawn into boards, dried, and sent to lumberyards for sale, the lumber isn't yet ready for use. The rough boards from the mill saw need to be surfaced, or smoothed and flattened. Their edges have to be jointed, or straightened. Sometimes the mill or lumberyard machine planes each side of the board until it reaches a certain thickness. The techniques they use, or drying, storage and weather conditions, result in lumber defects that have to be corrected before joinery begins.

Pictured here, the basic defects in lumber are cupping, bowing, crooking, and twisting. They all result from problems in the drying process that cause the board to warp out of a straight or flat plane.

Defects that aren't obvious to the eye are detected by placing a long steel straightedge across or along the board and sighting for a gap. The straightedge also checks the progress of surfacing and jointing once they're begun. Winding sticks are used to check for twisting. The perfectly straight and parallel sticks are placed at each end of a board and sighted across. They show whether a board is in winding (twisted) or out of winding (flat).

Dressing lumber is a process that removes material until the wood is smooth, flat, straight, and of the desired thickness. There are two choices for correcting defects to yield usable material. Which correction is used depends on the severity of the defect.

Mild defects are corrected by planing down high spots until the board is straight, flat, and to thickness. More severe defects require sawing the wood into shorter lengths or narrower widths before planing or jointing to minimize the defect so less material is wasted.

The process of dressing lumber is basically the same whether done by handtools or by machine. The first step, which flattens the face, is the most critical, whether jointer-handplaned or power-jointed, because the remaining steps reference from this face. Once the face is flattened, it should be marked as shown, and the first straightened edge also marked. These original surfaces are used to guide further processes like cutting or laying out joints.

Common Faults In Lumber

Rough lumber that hasn't been surface planed or edge jointed isn't smooth, flat, or straight and ready for building, which is often true even if it's dressed by the lumberyard.

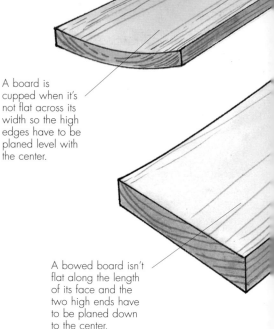

A board is cupped when it's not flat across its width so the high edges have to be planed level with the center.

A bowed board isn't flat along the length of its face and the two high ends have to be planed down to the center.

Preparing Rough Lumber by Hand

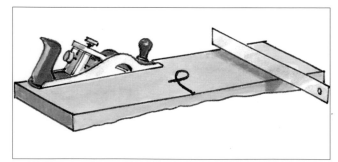

1 The board is trimmed somewhat over the shortest usable length and flattened on one face with scrub, jack, and jointer planes, then marked as flat.

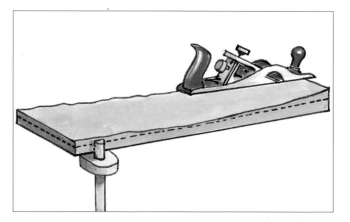

2 A marking gauge set to the desired thickness references off the flat face to mark a parallel line around the edges, and the second face is then planed down to it.

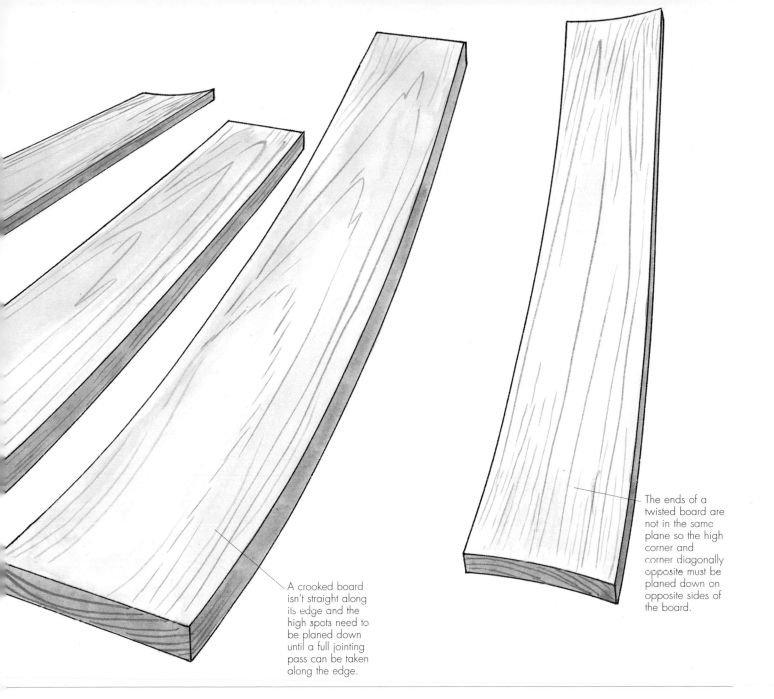

A crooked board isn't straight along its edge and the high spots need to be planed down until a full jointing pass can be taken along the edge.

The ends of a twisted board are not in the same plane so the high corner and corner diagonally opposite must be planed down on opposite sides of the board.

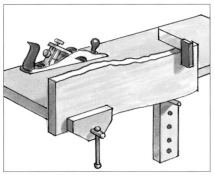

3 The board is put in a vise with the board's far end supported, then a jointer plane straightens the edge and makes it square to the face.

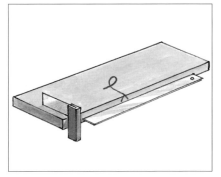

4 The straightened edge is marked pointing to the face it was squared from; now the edge can guide against the sawfence or reference another guideline for planing the board to width.

Winding Sticks

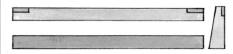

Winding sticks for detecting twist aren't commercially available but are made from straight stock profiled heavier at the bottom with a stained front stick and index marks on the back.

In use, winding sticks are placed across the board at opposite ends and lined up for sighting that shows a white mark between the sticks if the board is twisted.

Measuring and Marking

Measuring out a particular distance and marking it precisely onto wood is a simple task provided certain information is applied. This ensures that the fine tolerances of joinery (within the thickness of one or two business cards) are accurately laid out by the available tools.

Marking Tools

The lines made by different marking devices can vary in width and affect the accuracy of the layout.

Scribing knife makes finest line

Marking awl marks well with the grain

The basic tools for marking are the pencil, awl, and marking knife. As a pencil dulls, its line gets wider and less distinct, so the mark gets imprecise. An awl mark is consistently narrow, but the line is fuzzy when it's crossgrain. A marking knife makes the finest line possible so no slop in the joint is introduced.

A marking knife cleanly severs the top layer of wood fibers when it scribes crossgrain, which helps to prevent tear-out (losing bits of wood from the surface). It also leaves a tiny clean cut that helps guide tools. A good marking knife has a fine-tapered cross-section and a long tip to get into corners, like that on several of the chip carving knives.

Fine lines have no value unless they're precisely placed. Etched increments in a rule will locate the tip of a marking knife precisely at the increment. Holding a rule on edge so the increment contacts the wood avoids inaccuracies from an angled sight line.

Steel tapes and rules vary. Buying within one brand helps, especially if one tape is used for larger parts and a shorter, lighter one for the smaller work. Even then, check that the measurements from one match up to the other.

Marking and cutting gauges are layout tools that scribe a line parallel to a wood edge with a steel point or knife. A moveable fence adjusts the line's distance from the edge. Special mortise marking gauges scribe two parallel lines to help lay out the mortise and tenon or other joints. The distance between their two points is adjustable, and so is their fence. All these tools need to be fine tuned as shown. Care in their selection avoids the inconveniences of poor design that lead to difficult or inaccurate fence and point settings.

Pencil lines vary with sharpness

Incremental Markings

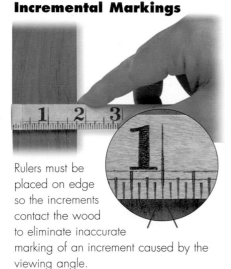

Rulers must be placed on edge so the increments contact the wood to eliminate inaccurate marking of an increment caused by the viewing angle.

1cm 2 3 4 5 6 7

Extend all metal tapes and rulers and compare whether their increments align and their lengths at full extension are the same.

Avoid wooden rules whose increments are painted rather than incised, as the increments themselves are too wide to be accurate.

Marking and Cutting Gauges

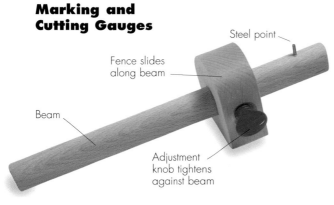

Steel point

Fence slides along beam

Beam

Adjustment knob tightens against beam

A basic marking gauge has a round steel point and adjustable fence that rides the wood's edge while the point marks a line a set distance from the edge.

A cutting gauge has a small knife wedged into the beam and is good for clean crossgrain scoring in addition to cutting narrow strips of veneer.

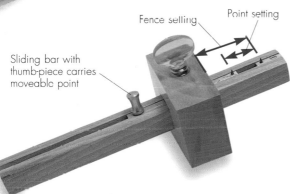

Fence setting   Point setting

Sliding bar with thumb-piece carries moveable point

The mortise gauge's fixed and moveable points mark parallel lines, but on this model, the fence and point settings both have to be held until one knob tightens them.

A thumbscrew moves the point up and down the beam but the screw adjustment that tightens the fence needs another tool to tighten it.

A thumbscrew on this gauge sets the distance between points, and a second knob tightens the fence setting to locate the parallel lines in the wood.

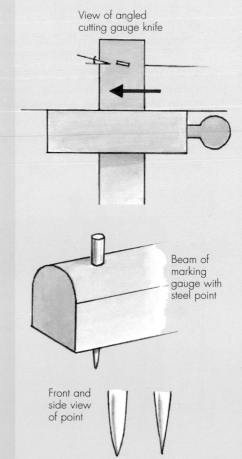

Beam of cutting gauge with knife and wedge

Commercial cutting and marking gauges need to be fine tuned to work smoothly. Some cutting gauges are shipped with the knife reversed so the bevel is on the wrong side. Remove either the knife or point and file it to the front view and profile shown, then reinsert the knife at a slight angle to protrude from the beam only about the thickness of a coin. The bevel side of the knife should be on the inside, toward the fence so any wood fibers it may crush are in the waste. As the gauge is pulled, the angle helps the knife to draw the fence of the gauge firmly against the wood.

View of angled cutting gauge knife

Beam of marking gauge with steel point

Front and side view of point

Keeping Order and Preventing Layout Errors

Woodworking projects generate a startling number of parts that need to be cut to size and kept sorted out. There are two layout and marking systems that make these tasks a breeze.

Using a Story Pole

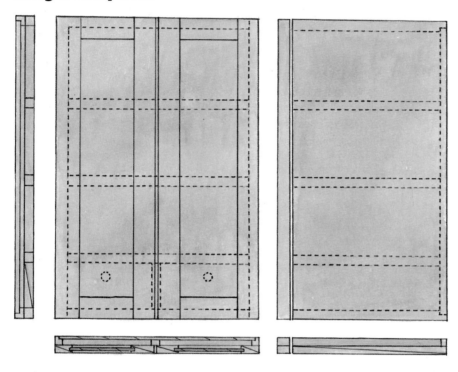

Work out proportions and construction details on full-size drawings and transfer them to story poles; then dimensions can be matched to the actual cabinet and help set up machines without measuring.

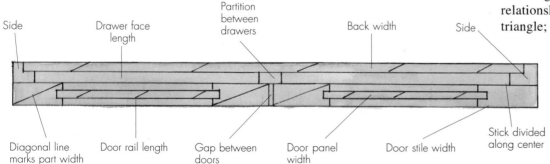

Side — Drawer face length — Partition between drawers — Back width — Side

Diagonal line marks part width — Door rail length — Gap between doors — Door panel width — Door stile width — Stick divided along center

A story pole on a stick carries an actual-size layout of the cabinet in section; part sizes and joinery are marked in either the horizontal or vertical plane.

A story pole is just a clean wood strip that is laid out from a full-sized drawing or used in place of one. It shows all the joinery, the parts, their sizes, and their location in a project in section. Each project will probably require a story pole for its vertical and horizontal planes, either on separate sticks or the back and front of one stick. Once the story pole is made and each part labeled on it, part sizes can be matched to it or their locations in the structure transferred from it to the actual assembly without using any other measure.

Story poles also speed repetitive marking tasks on many parts, like a bureau full of dovetailed drawers. A miniature story pole with the dovetail spacing marked out saves measuring it onto each drawer and risking mismeasuring here or there.

The system for identifying and sorting numerous and sometimes duplicate parts like the bureau drawers is equally simple. Triangle marking uses a few principles and an isosceles triangle which has sides of equal length to keep parts ordered.

Once a stack of drawer fronts, sides, and backs are cut, they are matched up for best grain. Mated parts are placed in the same relationship they'll have when assembled and, using a lumber crayon available in any hardware store, marked together with an isosceles triangle that always points up or away from the viewer. The two drawer sides are brought together in their assembled relationship and marked with a triangle; the front and back are similarly marked. Each part must carry two lines of the triangle.

Each set of duplicate parts, like sets of drawer sides, is marked with an additional line shared by mated parts, either a second baseline or an additional side line. So the second set of drawer sides has two baselines, the third three, and so on. It's easy to match and orient parts marked by this method.

Triangle Marking

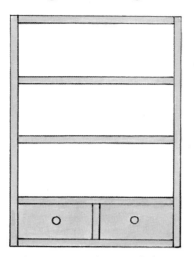

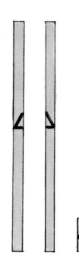

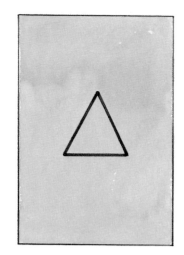

Cabinet interior showing shelves and drawers

The cabinet back, sides, top, bottom, and shelf parts are placed as in their position in the cabinet and marked by a triangle that always points up or away.

Parts that are marked with triangles pointing up or away are easy to spot when reversed or out of order.

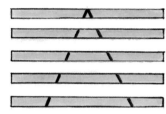

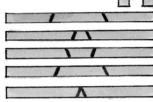

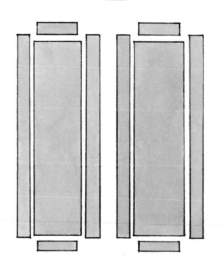

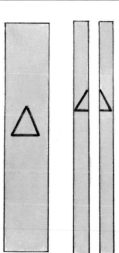

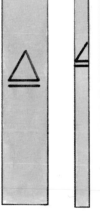

Cabinet doors exploded

An additional line on a triangle side distinguishes mated parts and helps orient each door's horizontal rails, vertical stiles, and panels for joinery layout and best grain.

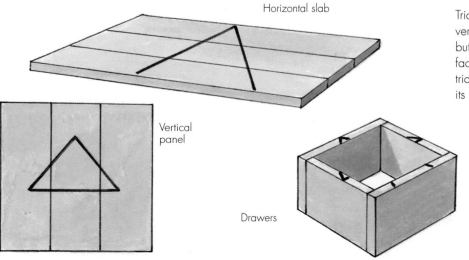

Horizontal slab

Vertical panel

Drawers

Triangles work on horizontal slabs, vertical panels, or drawers, but when joinery requires marking the faces of a leg set, each encircling triangle needs one more baseline than its neighbor.

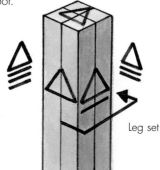

Leg set

Exact Clamping and Assembly

Despite good craftsmanship, the fit of joinery can be distorted by misdirected clamp forces. A great deal of time and energy has been invested by the time the parts are ready for gluing, but a little more patience spent on careful clamping pays off with a good return.

Parts will slip in wet glue or assemblies distort if the bearing surfaces of the clamps aren't flat to the wood, and the clamp's length not parallel to the nearest wood surface. The clamp force on wood is like pressing a finger into a sponge: the area around the pressure point may deflect. Then the joint's mating surfaces won't make contact for a good bond if the wood is too thin to distribute the force or too few clamps are used.

Clamping blocks cut from scrap help solve this problem by distributing the pressure and, in the process, prevent the clamp from marring the wood surface. But clamping blocks can create the same problem they are trying to solve if they aren't sized to the thickness, width, or area of the joint being glued.

Dry test the fit of all assemblies before any glue is applied. Last-minute refitting will be less messy or rushed by drying glue. This dry test gives a chance to decide the clamps needed, to cut clamping blocks, and to have the glue and other materials close at hand. Don't forget spreading rollers or brushes, waxed paper to insert between blocks and wood, and clean-up rags.

Once the parts are clamped, check the assembly for squareness while the wet glue still allows for adjustment. This is done by measuring the diagonals with a tape (and the help of a friend if the assembly is large). Instead of a tape, diagonal sticks can be used. These are two sticks made from straight stock, pointed at the ends to fit into the corners. They slide along each other's length in opposite directions until they reach into the corners, then are held together or marked across to compare that length to the remaining diagonal. Any difference in the measurements is corrected by readjusting the clamps until the diagonals measure the same and the assembly is square.

Distributing Pressure

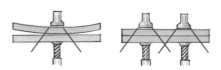

When the wood is thin or there aren't enough clamps, the pressure isn't distributed evenly and may cause the surrounding wood parts to separate.

Positioning Clamps

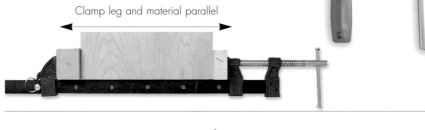

Pressure pads in line

The bearing surfaces of the clamps need to be flat to the wood and in line so pressure won't distort an assembly or cause it to slide out of position.

Clamp leg and material parallel

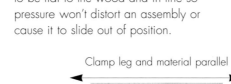

Checking Assemblies for Square

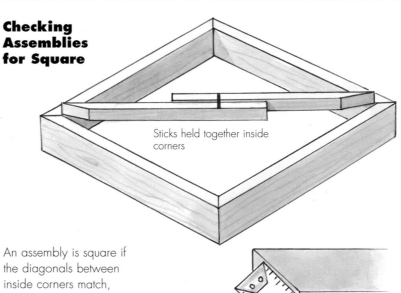

Sticks held together inside corners

An assembly is square if the diagonals between inside corners match, whether measured from the tape's inch mark to the corner diagonally opposite or by diagonal sticks extended between them.

Measure from inch mark diagonally to opposite inside corner

Sizing and Placing Blocks

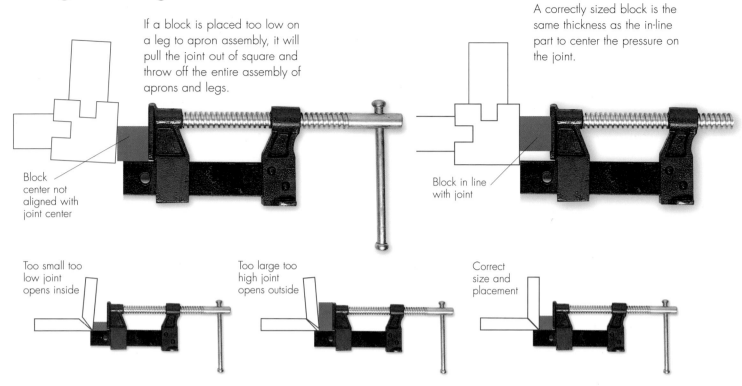

If a block is placed too low on a leg to apron assembly, it will pull the joint out of square and throw off the entire assembly of aprons and legs.

A correctly sized block is the same thickness as the in-line part to center the pressure on the joint.

Block center not aligned with joint center

Block in line with joint

Too small too low joint opens inside

Too large too high joint opens outside

Correct size and placement

Clamping blocks distribute the pressure and prevent marring, but a block that is too narrow and placed too low will open the joint on the side.

A thick block that extends above the thickness of the joint will push it in on itself and open the outside corner.

Raising the block brings the clamp pressure in line with the apron for a square assembly.

Correcting a Twisted Glue-Up

Correcting an Out of Square Glue-Up

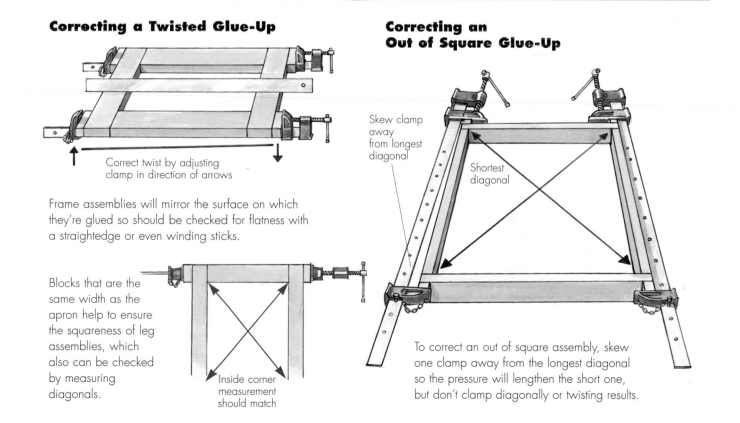

Correct twist by adjusting clamp in direction of arrows

Frame assemblies will mirror the surface on which they're glued so should be checked for flatness with a straightedge or even winding sticks.

Blocks that are the same width as the apron help to ensure the squareness of leg assemblies, which also can be checked by measuring diagonals.

Inside corner measurement should match

Skew clamp away from longest diagonal

Shortest diagonal

To correct an out of square assembly, skew one clamp away from the longest diagonal so the pressure will lengthen the short one, but don't clamp diagonally or twisting results.

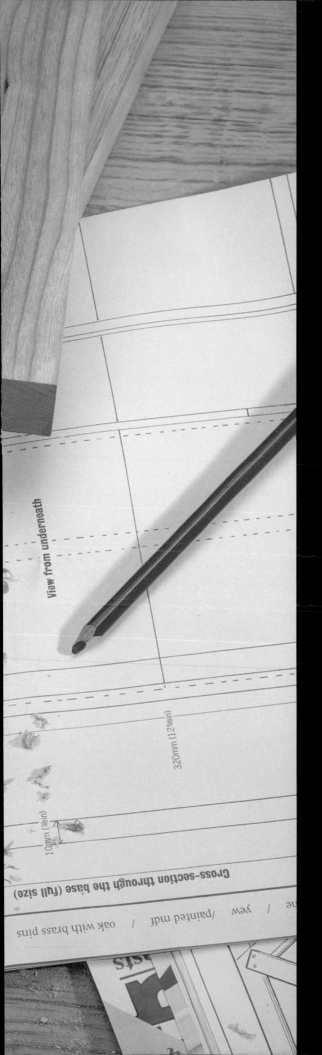

View from underneath

320mm (1.25⁸in)

10mm (³⁄₈in)

Cross-section through the base (full size)

oak with brass pins / yew /painted mdf/ ...ne / ...sts

CHAPTER TWO

DESIGNING JOINTS

The characteristics of the material, the configuration of the structure's parts, the anticipated stresses on the assembly, and aesthetics all contribute to the development of a joint design. In this chapter, the components of joinery are examined and all the important factors will be considered when creating the best joint for the design, material, and structure.

The Basic Orientations of Wood Parts

In any design, the parts meet in common configurations, and then ways to hold them together mechanically, with adhesive, or by a combination of the two are developed. The positional relationships of the parts are not in themselves joints, but certain families of joints and joint types evolve from these basic orientations to meet the requirements of the material, the structure, and aesthetics.

Parallel Orientation

Boards joined by their edges to increase overall wood width are in the parallel orientation. It permits using narrow stock, as well as the division and reassembly of wide stock to minimize checking and cupping. Parallel orientation also offers the flexibility to enhance design with grain patterns, which are more properly described as the wood's "figures." Butted, splined, and tongued joints, as well as dowels and biscuits, are commonly found here.

"I" Orientation

When wood is joined end to end, in the "I" orientation, the overall wood length is increased. Scarf joints have evolved from the "I" orientation. They are widely used in timber framing and were artistically developed in old-world Japan where long timber was in short supply. The scarf joint is common to boatbuilding, but it only occasionally appears in furniture, either in utility or in decoration.

"L" Orientation

The "L" orientation is the most common for carcase, corner, and framing joints. There are three ways wood can be joined in the "L" orientation: end to edge, end to face, and edge to face. Reinforced butts and miters, mortise and tenon, lap joints, box or finger joints, rabbets, the dovetail, and more are all generated at this corner.

"T" Orientation

Less prolific than the "L," the "T" orientation spawns mortise and tenon and lap joints, but is best remembered as the site of the housed joint, whether dadoed, rabbeted, or dovetailed. Here is where shelf ends and dividers slide into home. As in the "L" orientation, "T" joints can be end to edge, end to face, or edge to face.

Crossed Orientation

The crossed orientation has a small family of face-to-face lap joints to its name doing light-duty joining of frames. Chinese lattice work has made an art form of this orientation, as has the Japanese shoji screen. By contrast, the deeper edge lap has limited use and refinement. It is primarily seen in knock-down plywood construction or in egg-crated drawer dividers.

Angled Orientation

The angled orientation acts as a modifier to the other orientations. It picks and chooses members from various joint families as it mixes with each positional orientation, changing the joining angle to anything other than 90 degrees or 180 degrees. Consequently we have such joints as the oblique scarf, angled lap, and barrel stave construction.

The joints listed (Right) can be developed if the wood you are working with is in the orientation shown.

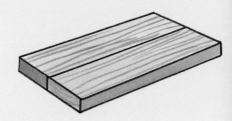

Parallel Orientation

Butted edge joint	Shiplap
Spline joint	Tongue and bead
Rubbed joint	V-groove
Tongue and groove	

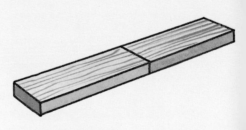

I Orientation

End-to-end scarf	Rabbet scarf
Edge-to-edge scarf	Transverse keyed scarf
Squint-butted scarf	

Crossed Orientation

Top view:	Center lap
	Cogged lap
Bottom view:	Edge lap

L Orientation

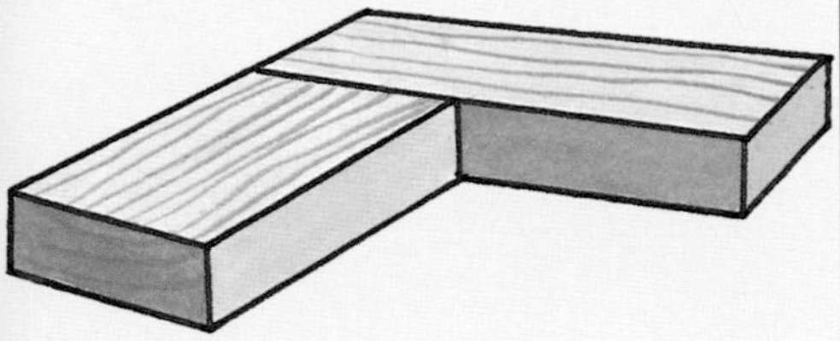

End lap
Mortise and tenon
Miter joint

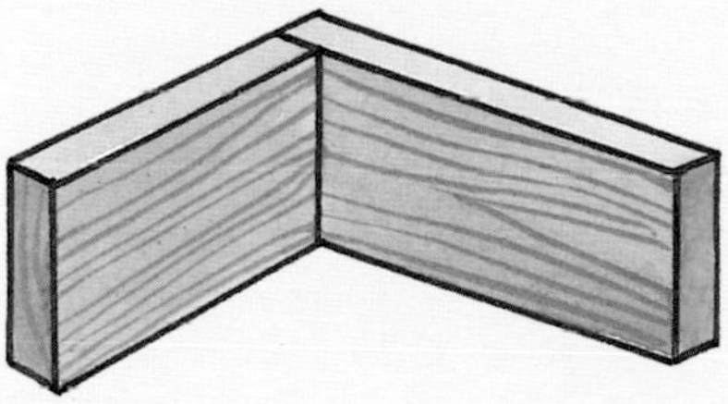

Dovetails
Lock miter
Fingerlap joint

Offset tongue and groove
Rabbet miter

T Orientation

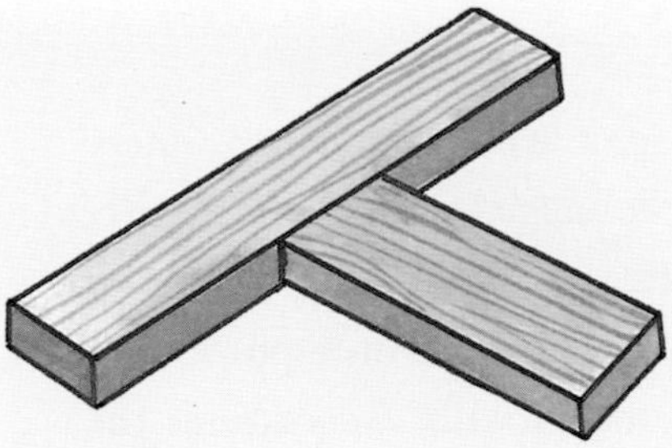

Center lap
Dovetail lap
Mortise and tenon

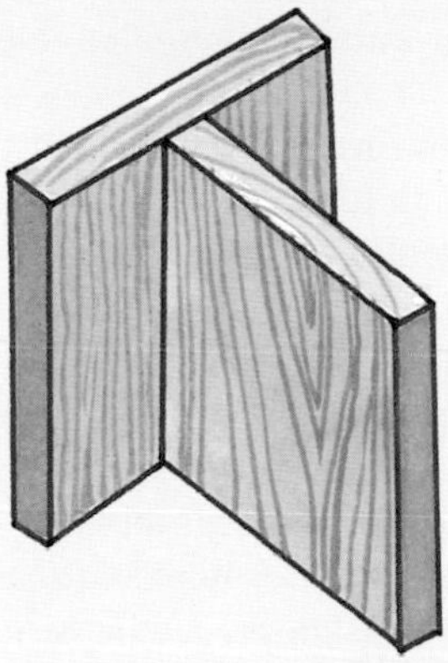

Sliding dovetail
Tongue and groove

Housed rabbet
Housed sliding dovetail

Angled Orientation

Angled mortise and tenon
Angled center lap
Loose tenon

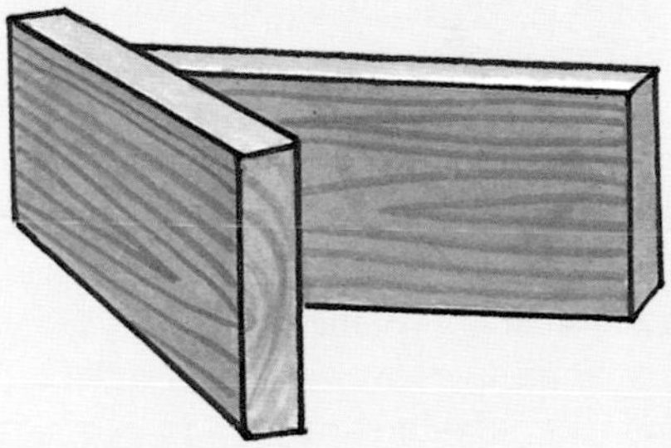

Splined bevel joint
Biscuit joint
Angled sliding dovetail

Bevel joint
Splined bevel joint

The Basic Elements of Joinery

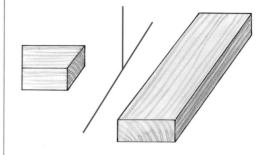

ach woodworking joint is a combination of at least two basic joinery elements. Two of these elements are mated and mechanically interlock or create glue surfaces that "join" two parts. As joinery gets more complex, the basic elements are modified and enhanced to improve joint strength or design, but these basic components will always form the building blocks of a joint.

Square cuts result when the blade angle is 90 degrees to the wood surface and the blade path runs 90 degrees to the entrance end or edge of the wood.

Elements or cuts fall roughly into two categories. Sawn elements can be completed by one cut on the wood's end or edge by a hand or power saw. Milled elements are part of a step by step process. It begins with sizing the part, then removing material to leave a milled element's characteristic shape cut into the wood.

A sawn element, either square, angled, or compound angled, is butted to its complementary cut to make width joints, mitered corners, six-sided boxes, or cone shapes, to name some examples. Sawing is the quickest and most common method to give the wood ends or edges these shapes, but it isn't the only method. Hand planing, power jointing, or routing are alternatives.

Milled elements or cuts are the L-shaped rabbet, variously shaped pockets or sockets, and U-shaped groove, dado, and edge dado or notch. These flat-bottomed U-shaped cuts are distinguished by whether they parallel the grain (groove), cross the grain (dado), or cut into the board's edge (notch). Different joint families combine these elements with other cuts to form joints suited to the design. The square cut and pocket yield a mortise and tenon joint for joining aprons to legs. A dado and square cut give us the housing joint for shelves. A rabbet and a dado create a lap joint for T-joining wood parts, and so on.

There is an infinite number of approaches to making milled cuts, and even the sawn ones. No single tool or method is the only option to making these components of joints. In fact, knowing how to make them by a variety of tools and means, how to modify them, and how to combine them effectively with other elements is what joinery is all about.

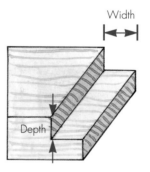

An L-shaped step cut in the end or edge of the wood is called a rabbet, whose depth and width are varied as needed.

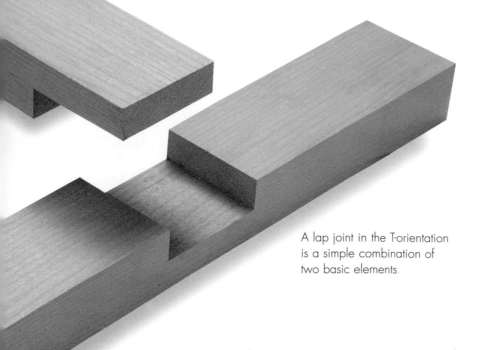

A lap joint in the T-orientation is a simple combination of two basic elements.

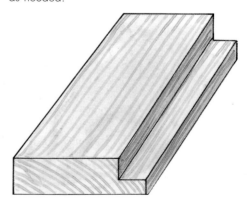

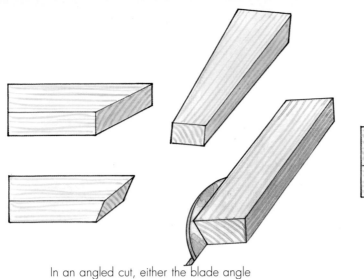

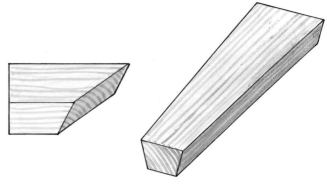

In an angled cut, either the blade angle is not 90 degrees to the wood surface or the blade path doesn't run 90 degrees to the entrance plane.

In a compound angle, both the blade angle and blade path are not 90 degrees, but are any other angle or combination of blade angle and blade path.

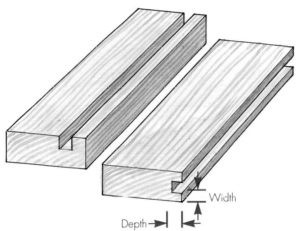

Width
Depth

Grooves are flat-bottomed U-shaped cuts that always run parallel to the grain in the face or edge of the wood.

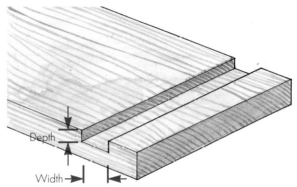

Depth
Width

A dado is also a U-shaped flat-bottomed cut like a groove, but dadoes only run across the grain and if cut wide are sometimes called trenches.

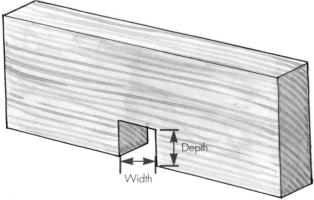

Depth
Width

A dado cut into the edge of a board is called a notch or edge dado and is usually deeper than a dado cut in the board face.

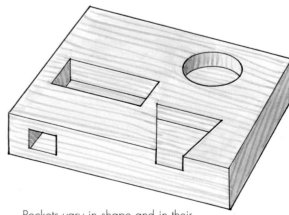

Pockets vary in shape and in their location in the board, have specialized names, and serve different joinery purposes, which are covered in following chapters.

Wood Material and Joint Design

The most important fact to keep in mind when designing wood joinery is that solid wood is not dimensionally stable. The cell structure of wood can be likened simplistically to a bundle of straws, which adsorb and desorb water vapor in response to changes in the relative humidity to maintain moisture equilibrium with the environment. This constant fluctuation of the wood's moisture content results in expansion and contraction across the width of grain and a negligible change in length. Unless this phenomenon is addressed by design, it's possible for wood movement to destroy a joint or the material itself.

Movement in wood varies by species, by its classification as hardwood or softwood and between the heartwood and sapwood of each tree.

Grain and Wood Movement

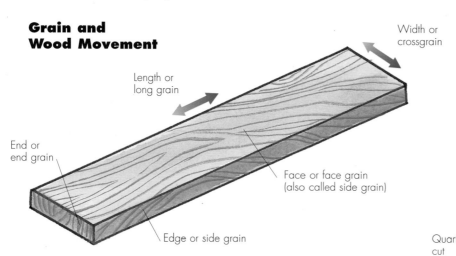

Width or crossgrain

Length or long grain

End or end grain

Face or face grain (also called side grain)

Edge or side grain

Predicting Wood Movement

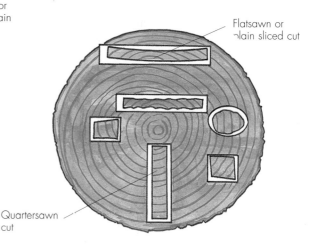

Flatsawn or plain sliced cut

Quartersawn cut

Lumber cuts from the log shrink and expand most along the outer growth rings visible in their end grain pattern.

Movement

Wood movement becomes a danger to joinery when the long grain of one part is joined across the grain of another, and dimensional conflict is created. This situation is found in some of the "L," "T," and crossed positions where the long grains of two parts meet at right angles.

Movement in wood varies by species, by its classification as hardwood or softwood, and between the heartwood and sapwood of each tree. Specialized books detail the specific characteristics of wood by genus and species, including stability. However, in general, the key to predicting wood movement lies in the end grain of each board.

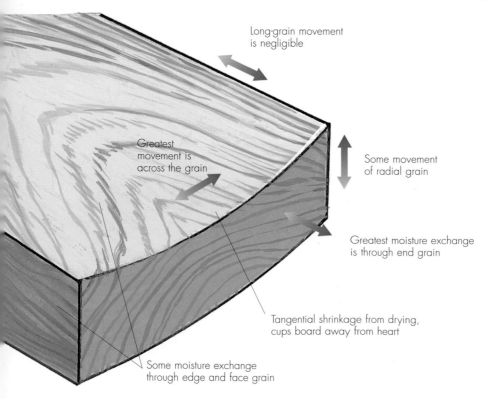

Long-grain movement is negligible

Greatest movement is across the grain

Some movement of radial grain

Greatest moisture exchange is through end grain

Tangential shrinkage from drying, cups board away from heart

Some moisture exchange through edge and face grain

In relation to the growth rings of the tree, wood moves more tangentially than radially, or more along the rings than across them. As wet wood dries, greater tangential shrinkage distorts the board consistent with its original position in the log. That position is easy to determine by the pattern of growth rings in a board's end grain.

The most common flatsawn boards are cut from the log so the growth rings on the end run more parallel to the width than the thickness of the board. Quartersawn boards are cut so growth rings are more perpendicular to the width of the board. A quick rule of thumb is that a flatsawn board in most species will shrink about twice as much across its width as a quartersawn board, and consequently have twice the potential for expansion and dimensional instability.

Grain

Wood material also has strengths and weaknesses of grain that affect joinery design. With effort, wood can be broken across the grain, but the likelier breakage is along the grain when wood is left too thin or when weak "short grain" created by milling can't hold the material together. Conscientious design can reduce or eliminate all these problems.

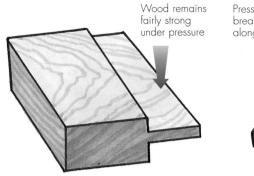
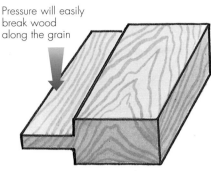

Wood remains fairly strong under pressure

Pressure will easily break wood along the grain

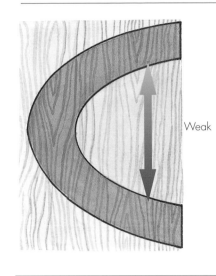
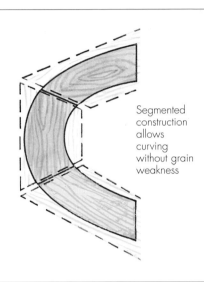

Weak

Segmented construction allows curving without grain weakness

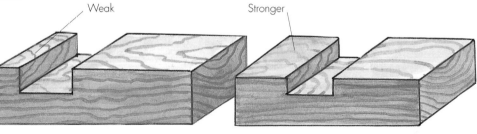

Weak

Stronger

The depth of the cut shouldn't be more than the width of the remaining end

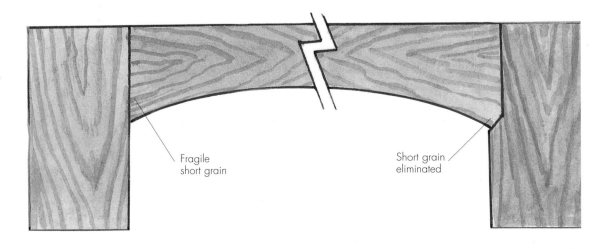

Wood is fragile when the grain runs across a point created by a curved cut; a different joint design reduces the danger of breakage in arched door frames.

Fragile short grain

Short grain eliminated

Strategies for Accommodating Wood Movement

Align grain to unify movement

Continuing the long grain around a carcass unifies wood movement. Keeping long grain vertical on the sides prevents shrinkage from binding doors. Running long grain across the bottom keeps shrinkage from tightening drawers.

Cabinet expands and contracts across the grain as a unit

Design crossgrain joints to eliminate conflict

The mechanical interlock of a sliding dovetail holds the breadboard end of a tabletop without glue. One central pin keeps the end aligned as the top moves freely with changes in humidity.

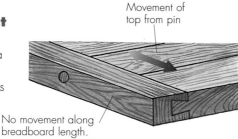

Movement of top from pin

No movement along breadboard length.

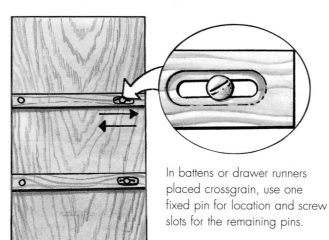

In battens or drawer runners placed crossgrain, use one fixed pin for location and screw slots for the remaining pins.

Use the best of classic designs

Classic drawer design attaches a solid bottom to the front groove only. This allows wide grain to expand under the low back while air can escape over it to avoid pistoning when closing.

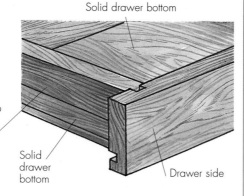

Solid drawer bottom

Lower drawer back

Solid drawer bottom

Drawer side

Strategies for Minimizing Wood Movement

Arrange grain to reduce movement

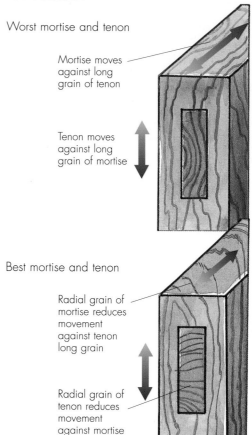

Worst mortise and tenon

Mortise moves against long grain of tenon

Tenon moves against long grain of mortise

Best mortise and tenon

Radial grain of mortise reduces movement against tenon long grain

Radial grain of tenon reduces movement against mortise long grain

Strategies for Restraining Wood Movement

Divide and conquer

Glue will restrain wood movement if the glue surface area in the joint is high in relation to the wood thickness.

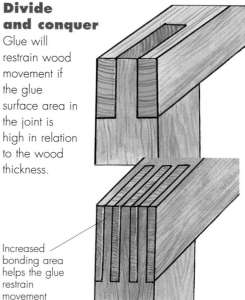

Increased bonding area helps the glue restrain movement

Select a stable species or cut

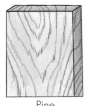

Pine   Rosewood   Plain cut   Quartersawn cut

An 18-inch width of new-growth pine can move as much as ⅜ inch more than a similar width of rosewood.

Generally the width of plain sliced or flatsawn lumber moves about twice the amount as quartersawn lumber of the same species.

Finish all sides equally to balance movement and reduce extremes of moisture exchange

Wood finished on only one side will cup from imbalanced moisture exchange with the environment.

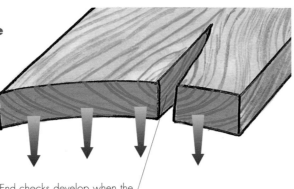

End checks develop when the unsealed end grain gives off moisture and shrinks more than the rest of the board

Play forces against each other

The alternating grain direction in layers of plywood combine to form a stable material. For information on wood movement and glue, see the section Glues and Gluing on pages 32–33.

When the walls of tubular wood cells adsorb moisture from the environment and try to swell while restrained (as they are in cross-grain joints with dimensional conflict), the structure of the material becomes stressed. The width can't expand when taking on extra moisture in the cell walls, and the cells themselves are compressed instead. After the compressed cells desorb the moisture from their walls, the cumulative compression of each cell making up the width causes the wood to shrink back to less than its original size, and the joint thus loosens.

Choosing a Joint

One school of thought says a craftsperson should design around the construction; another says to construct around the design. In reality, both methods interact. The design dictates the possible joints or is modified so joints which will overcome the structure's weaknesses can be used.

Before the basic orientations of wood are joined and put into service in a structure, the forces the joints have to resist in any design need to be analyzed. This doesn't require an engineering degree, just an awareness of the mechanical stresses on joints and some joinery solutions to them. Like problems with dimensional conflict, potential problems from stresses on an assembly in use are easy to predict and solve with an appropriate joint.

Utility, economy, and the work's aesthetic priorities all influence the choice of joinery for a design. Certain styles seem to exist just to showcase well-crafted joinery, while in others an overall look predominates and assembly techniques are hidden. Elaborate joinery is time consuming and not always necessary for structure nor economically justified for function. The wide range of visible and invisible joints can accommodate every taste.

Joinery combined with lumber selection can show wood grain and figure to advantage as the focus of a design, as an important element, or reduce an excess of the grain's visual distraction in the overall piece. Economy again tempers aesthetics when matched lumber is scarce as certain logging cuts waste more lumber in the milling process and are therefore more expensive.

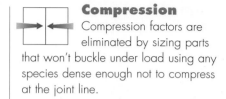

Compression

Compression factors are eliminated by sizing parts that won't buckle under load using any species dense enough not to compress at the joint line.

Table weight compresses upright and foot

Shear

Shear forces can be a factor when there is insufficient material for loading, but usually shear refers to push/pull stress on a glue line. Such stress can be relieved mechanically by joinery, pins, or reinforcing screws.

Scarf joint

Tension tries to shear glue line

Cogged joint

Locking spline reduces stress

Stresses on Joints

Tension

Tension is best overcome by mechanical resistance to the force pulling the joint apart. This can be either as an inherent feature of the joint or one added by wedging or pinning.

Tension

Weight of contents

Through dovetail

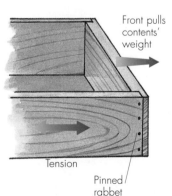

Front pulls contents' weight

Tension

Pinned rabbet

Blind mortise and tenon

Through wedged mortise and tenon

The pedestal as seen from below shows how the dovetail tenons lock the legs in place to relieve shear stress

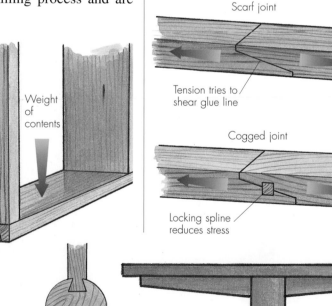

The table's weight puts shear stress on the glue line of the leg tenons

Bending or Racking

The resistance of individual joints to bending can be increased, as can the rigidity against joints bending in unison called racking.

A single-shouldered blind tenon can be made more rigid by adding a second shoulder, dividing the tenon into two, or running a single tenon full depth and wedging it

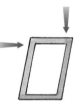

A back, bottom or face frame minimizes racking in box structures.

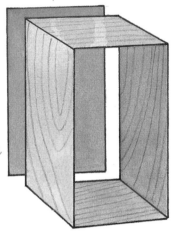

Without reinforcement, open box shape is unstable

Apron too narrow to prevent racking

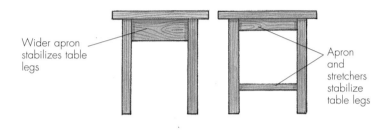

Adding or increasing frame structures in a table, such as deeper aprons or stretchers between the legs, will also combat racking

Wider apron stabilizes table legs

Apron and stretchers stabilize table legs

Joinery Style

By hiding or articulating the same basic joint, the "look" of a piece can change dramatically.

A tusked tenon is articulated to emphasize joinery

A blind mortise and tenon is blended by sculpting

Joinery and Grain Pattern

Edge joints combined with arrangements of matched lumber yield a variety of visual effects.

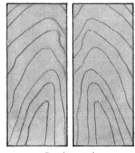

Slip match   Book match

How lumber matches are taken from the log

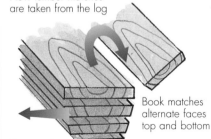

Book matches alternate faces top and bottom

Slip matches keep the same face always up

The waterfall, a length bevel joint cut from one board, continues the grain pattern over an angle

Both the chosen joint and how the wood was cut from the log alter the visual effect of these door frames

Butted   Mitered

Flat cut

 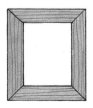

Quarter-sawn

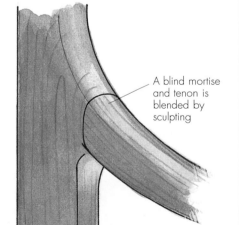

Glues and Gluing

Classifying glue by what it is made from (animal, vegetable, or mineral materials) is not as important as classifying by how the glue cures, either by solvent evaporation, chemical reaction, or heat setting. Woodworkers who know these processes can manipulate them to prolong assembly time or speed up drying. For example, when the solvent that is evaporating is water, temporary swelling or warping from introduced moisture can be planned for, avoided, or even chosen, as is a requirement for successful biscuit joinery.

Gluing science is complex, but for woodworking it can be reduced to basics. A handful of glues will handle most general needs, and a handful more the specialized ones. Situations for other than a general purpose glue are gluing oily, resinous, or particularly dense woods; gluing for a damp or wet environment; bonding non-porous materials like stone or metal to wood; instant bonding for modelmaking or repairs; bent laminating, which requires a non-plastic glue that won't flow or stretch under tension; assembly requiring reversibility of the bond for anticipated repairs; or needing a long "open" time for a complicated glue-up.

Long-grain contact

Cavity (glue)

Glue joins the long grains of a mortise and tenon; a cavity at the bottom collects the excess.

Wood Grain and Bond Strength

End grain glued to any other grain has much reduced bond strength, so butted joints should rely on joinery to create long-grain contact between the parts.

Long grain glued parallel to long grain makes a bond as strong as the wood itself, but cross-gluing it, while strong, creates dimensional conflict.

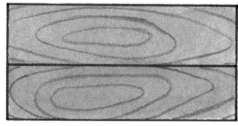

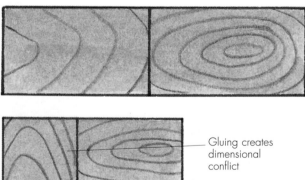

Gluing creates dimensional conflict

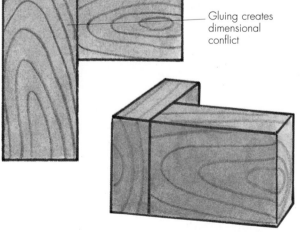

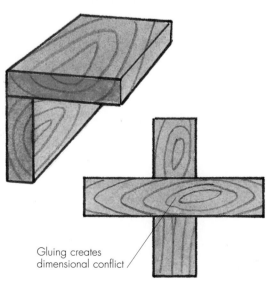

Gluing creates dimensional conflict

Application and Clamping

The idea of gluing is to create a continuous adhesive film between the mating parts and hold them in it until the glue dries and cures enough for safe handling. Some glues don't develop full bond strength for days. The amount of glue to spread, the spreading method, the time open before clamping, the clamping time, the drying time, and the cure time are all so varied by type and brand that the manufacturer's label or technical support line are the best resorts. But one rule of thumb is that soft woods are easier to glue than woods whose density makes glue penetration difficult and with over-clamping can squeeze the glue too thin.

Grain Orientation

Grain orientation for gluing is as important as it is in joint design because the glue bond is strong where there is long-grain to long-grain contact, and weak at any point of end grain contact. Glues help to restrain movement and so contribute to the internal stresses of wood when its moisture content fluctuates. In joints that are glued crossgrain, dimensional conflict and constant wood movement, however minute, stress the glue line. Over time, the combination of tiny constant stresses and the shrinkage of the wood from compression and drying can contribute to an eventual breakdown of the glue bond or material and loosen a joint. Finishing, particularly with films like varnish and polyurethane, can greatly reduce moisture penetration to protect the glue.

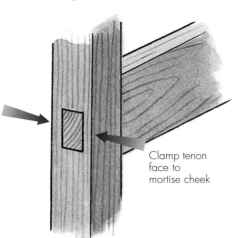

Clamp tenon face to mortise cheek

Glue Moisture and Joinery

Water-based glues swell the wood at the glue line. If the joint is planed flush before the glue's moisture has dissipated, subsequent moisture loss causes the joint to shrink.

Clamping for Best Bond

All surfaces of a joint should be pulled in snugly, but the direction of clamp pressure is best applied where it enables long-grain contact for the strongest glue bond.

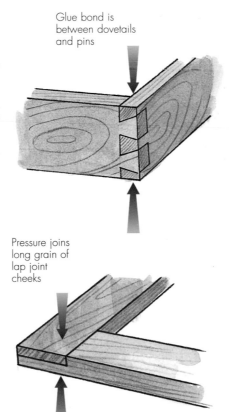

Glue bond is between dovetails and pins

Pressure joins long grain of lap joint cheeks

Wrong Moisture Content

If the moisture content of a project's wood isn't similar to that of its final environment, climatic change could damage the project. As moisture in the air increases or decreases, it could cause joints that fit on assembly to shrink or expand more than the glue or material can withstand. Such changes in humidity can also cause surfaces to cup or check. This applies as much to wood assembled in a damp basement and brought to a centrally heated second floor as it does to tropical furniture moved to the desert. Some glues won't set up properly or achieve full strength if the moisture content of the wood is too wet or too dry for bonds to form.

Bad Surface Preparation

Modern gluing theory prescribes that fresh and cleanly shaven mating surfaces must make full, flat contact for the continuous film of a good glue bond to form. High spots inside the joint prevent full contact, as do low spots that allow the glue to "pool." The hairiness of rough-sawn surfaces breaks the glue film and makes joints harder to pull up tight for an invisible glue line. Dull planer knives produce a glazed surface that doesn't glue well, and exotic woods have surface chemicals that require special glues or wiping down with acetone for a good bond.

Glue Chart

	PVA (white glue)	ALIPHATIC RESIN (yellow glue)	DRY HIDE GLUE	POLYURETHANE	RESORCINOL FORMALDEHYDE
Wood and wood materials	Yes	Yes	Yes	Yes	Yes
Non-porous materials	No	No	Yes	Yes	No
Preparation or mixing	No	No	Yes	No	Yes
Cure method	Solvent evaporation	Solvent evaporation	Solvent evaporation	Moisture catalyzed	Catalyzation
Open time	Avg	Avg	High	Avg	High
Clamp time	Avg	Avg	None to avg	Avg	High
Water resistant	No	No	No	Yes	Yes
Waterproof	No	No	No	Yes	Yes
Sandable	No: Gums up	Yes	Yes	Yes	Yes: Dust toxic
Gap-filling	No	No	Yes	No	Yes
Reversible/repairable	Yes	No	Yes	No	No
Thermoplastic (creeps)	Yes	Yes	No	No	No
Bonds oily or resinous wood	Yes*	Yes*	Yes*	Yes	Yes*
Water clean-up	Yes	Yes	Yes	No	Yes
Solvent clean-up	No	No	No	Yes	No
Cost	Low	Low	Low	Moderate	High
Health/safety concerns	No	No	No	Potential skin sensitivity Fumes	Formaldehyde Gas fumes

• not for structural bonds; * with acetone wash; † water-based type only

UREA FORMALDEHYDE (plastic resin)	EPOXY RESIN	CYANOACRYLATE (super glue)	CONTACT CEMENT
Yes	Yes	Yes	Yes•
No	Yes	Yes	Yes
Yes	Yes	No	No
Catalyzation	Catalyzation	Moisture catalyzed	Solvent evaporation
High	High	None – seconds	High
High	High	Temporary immobilisation	None
Yes	Yes	Yes	Yes
No	Yes	No	No
Yes: Dust Toxic	Yes: Difficult	Yes	No
No	Yes	Yes	No
No	No	No	Yes
No	No	No	Yes
No	Yes	Yes	No
Yes	No	No	Yes†
No	Yes	Yes	Yes
Moderate	High	Very high	High
Formaldehyde Gas fumes	Toxic until dry Irritant	Bonds skin Eye irritant	Toxic fumes Flammable

Bad Clamping

Excessive clamping force can rack well-fitted parts out of position or squeeze the glue film too thin. Dry parts should fit hand-tight on test assembly. Fits that need heavy pounding for dry assembly will be difficult to assemble when wet and leave little room for glue. They risk glue starvation or pistoning glue inside the joint and splitting the wood. Bad fits need to be corrected prior to glue-up to discourage excessive clamp force. Uneven clamping, either clamps spaced too far apart or the force not distributed with blocks placed under the pads, has an effect like sticking a finger into a sponge: the glue makes contact at the pressure spot and the remaining material rises away.

Wrong Adhesive

The choice of adhesive is dictated by the moisture and temperature extremes of the intended environment, the type of construction plus the load that will be placed on it, and the species of wood or any non-porous materials being glued to it. Secondary considerations are the glue's working properties (how long it can stay "open" before clamping, its dry and cure times, and working temperature sensitivities), plus cost. Careful research before gluing is the best defense.

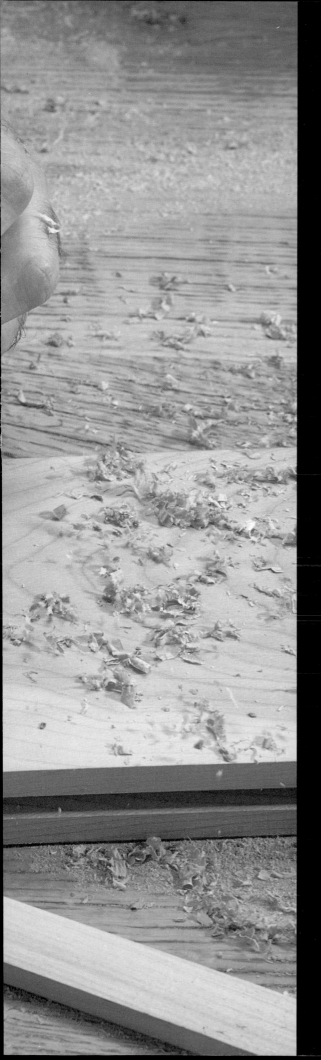

CHAPTER THREE

WIDTH AND LENGTH JOINTS

The purpose of width and length joints, also called edge and scarf joints, is to join individual boards into one wider or longer unit. There is little dimensional conflict, and because the parallel grain direction of their bonding surfaces makes a glue bond as strong as the wood itself, these joints require no interlocking joinery. However, there are methods to interlock such joints to reinforce them against certain types of stress, improve aesthetics, increase the gluing surface, or assist alignment and reduce slippage during gluing. But these refinements are just icing on an already substantial cake.

About Edge Joints

Unfortunately, edge joints are not entirely free from problems of wood movement. However, these problems relate more to the elements of the whole than to the joints themselves. For example, there are a number of considerations for gluing up panels or slabs. When gluing up a slab, whether to place all boards heartwood face up or alternate them up and down is a matter of preference and debate among woodworkers. Greater moisture loss at the ends of the boards can cause shrinking, splitting, or joint failure and is overcome by the finish or a "sprung" joint. An assembled panel's ends are automatically hidden in frame-and-panel construction, but on a table or other top, adding an aesthetic or stabilizing lipping at the ends requires careful thought, because it introduces crossgrain construction

A contrasting spline makes a decorative edge joint.

Wood Movement and Edge Joint Gluing

Edge-joined boards with heartwood sides up move as a unit, but boards alternating heartwood up and down cup oppositely and create a washboard effect that is harder to hold down.

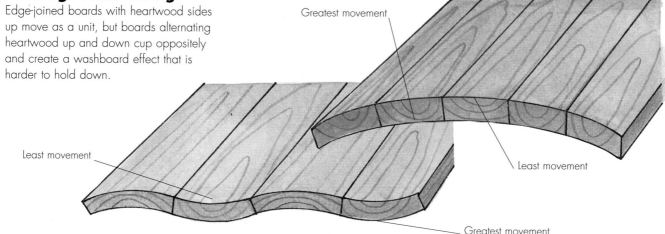

Greatest movement

Least movement

Least movement

Greatest movement

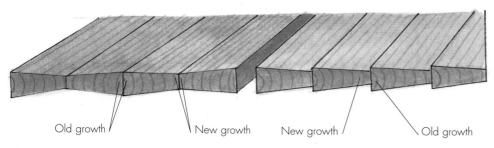

Old growth

New growth

New growth

Old growth

Older growth from the center of the tree and the newer growth of the outer rings shrink and expand differently when edge joined, creating drawbacks, usually minor in practice.

Under clamps, the 1/32" hollow of a sprung joint presses ends tightly, anticipating moisture loss so end shrinkage relieves tension on the wood and glue instead of creating it.

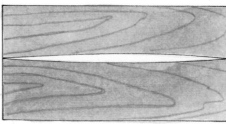

Special Jigs for Straight Edges and Tapers

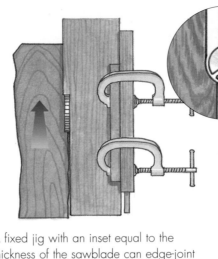

Laminate added to outfeed fence on a router table

A fixed jig with an inset equal to the thickness of the sawblade can edge-joint a board, as can a router table with a slight fence offset.

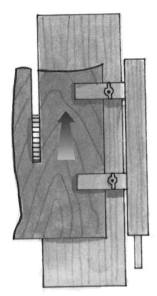

Fasten a crooked board overhanging a sliding plywood carriage to straighten the edge on a table saw.

Cut is stopped at wood push block

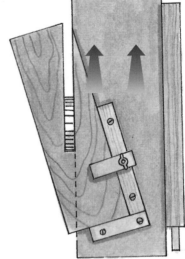

To taper-cut or waste at the leading end, align the marked taper with a carriage's edge and attach a fence or notch the carriage to fit the board's outline.

An adjustable taper jig has high wooden legs, a hinge, a sliding adjuster with wingnut, a handle, and a wood push block for safe cuts to the inside corner.

Clamping Width Joints

Edge clamping doesn't require expensive clamps, but cross clamping requires measures to keep the panel flat, such as alternating clamps top and bottom or using a handscrew or temporary battens at the ends.

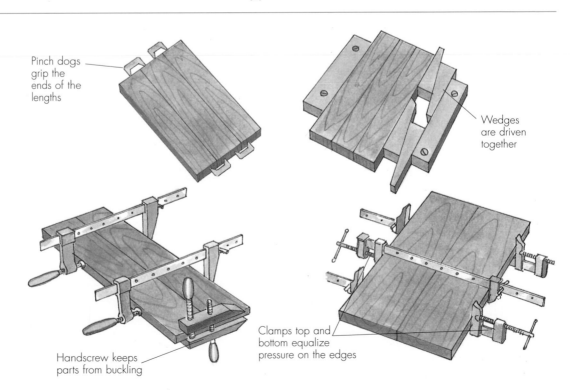

Pinch dogs grip the ends of the lengths

Wedges are driven together

Handscrew keeps parts from buckling

Clamps top and bottom equalize pressure on the edges

Simple and Reinforced Edge Joints

Plain Butt Glue Joint

A butted edge joint is strong enough for the majority of glue-ups for width. It's one of the few edge joints that can be "sprung," or pre-tensioned so later end grain shrinkage doesn't pull the joint apart. All this joint requires is flat, straight lumber, so the key to success is knowing how to accurately surface and dimension lumber by hand or with power tools.

Splined Joint

Splining is a quick and easy way to reinforce a width joint. If referenced from the marked face, it takes little calculation or layout for an accurate joint with perfect alignment of the faces. Splining also prevents slippage until the glue has dried. Double splines in thick lumber are equally simple to reference from both faces.

Man-made materials work well for splines. Exactly sized masonite is the easiest to match to standard cutter widths. Less-accurate plywood might require two grooving passes with an undersized cutter for a good fit. Thickness solid wood splines to match the cutter or widen the groove to fit available spline stock within the limits of joint proportions.

Rip splines slightly less wide than double the groove depth so the joint can close. Use stock that fits hand tight in the groove so the groove isn't forced open to the detriment of gluing contact with the spline. Grain in solid wood splines should run across the spline or diagonal for strength. For this reason, splines cut from solid wood are limited in length by the board's width and it takes several splines to equal the single continuous length possible from manmade materials where grain direction is not an issue. Be sure to test for fit in a test groove.

Machined Locking Edge

A single glue joint cutter makes each part of a locking edge joint in one pass. Alternate boards are flipped for milling so precise set-up and testing is necessary to get the faces of the mating edges flush. This joint makes the most sense for work in volume where there isn't time to fuss over multiple glue-ups.

Capped Spline

This variation is a cosmetic feature that gives an impression of quality and conscientious detailing. It isn't necessary to glue the cap to the spline, but to simplify assembly, first calculate the spline length. Then make it up by gluing two strips of the cap material to the edges of the spline material. Finally, rip full-length splines from it.

Stopped Spline

Routing for splines with a ballbearing spline cutter makes it easy to stop the groove on a mark to hide the splines. It's worth the price of a spline cutter to avoid making a stopped cut on the tablesaw, which is a risky and cumbersome procedure. Routing for splines saves lumber handling, too.

Plain Butt Glue Joint

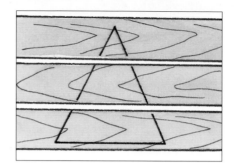

1 Rip stock to within ¼" of final width, then cut to length or leave enough for trimming after glue-up, arrange for grain pattern, and mark for position.

4 Clamp mated edges together and take a light shaving just to remove mill marks, or use a short sole to plane in a ¹⁄₃₂" hollow for a sprung joint.

Splined Joint

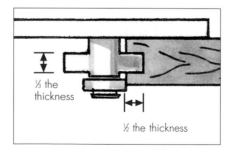

1 With a router registering from the marked face of each board, run a groove in the center of each edge to a depth of about ½ the wood thickness.

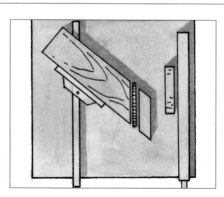

2 Match spline material thickness to the groove width of about ⅓ to ½ the stock thickness, then double the grooving depth and rip crossgrain strips just under it.

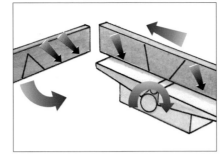

2 Once rough ripping reduces stock for better control, trim each edge to final dimension, alternating mating boards up and down to cancel any out-of-square in the blade setting.

3 For final dimensioning on the jointer, always feed stock to cut with the grain to avoid tear-out. Don't alternate faces to cancel out-of-square; set a precise fence to allow jointing for best grain direction.

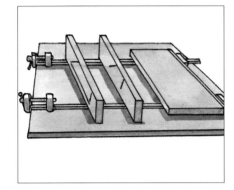

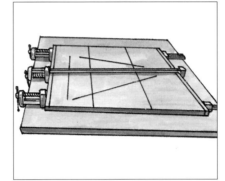

5 Set out the clamps on a flat surface and assemble the boards, checking for fit; then stand boards on edge to spread glue and clamp with battens protecting the edges.

6 Align the threaded screw with the board edge and counteract bowing with clamps on both sides; tighten clamps alternately so the assembly doesn't pop apart, then let dry and trim ends square.

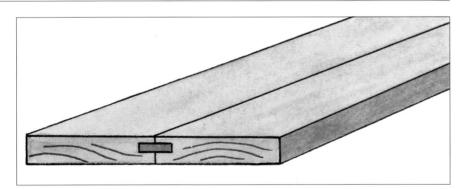

3 Test for fit: splines too wide prevent closing; tight ones could stress the groove when swollen by glue moisture. Spread glue on lips and in grooves, assemble, and clamp.

Machined Locking Edge

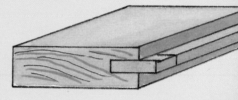

A glue joint cutter used in a router or router table increases the gluing surface and keeps boards aligned during glue-up.

Capped Spline

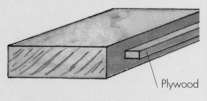

When the joint runs through and shows on the finished piece, a capped spline improves the appearance of a plywood spline or creates an effect with matching or contrasting wood.

Stopped Spline

Plywood

A stopped spline keeps the joinery hidden, or holds the spline back so further work like shaping the edge doesn't expose it.

Tongue and Groove

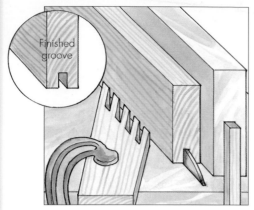

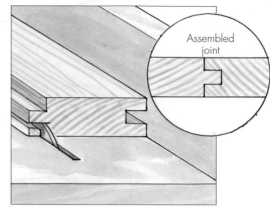

1 Raise a raker-toothed blade to ½ the stock thickness, set the fence to ⅓ the thickness from the blade, make one grooving pass, reverse the board so the second pass widens the groove.

2 Lower the blade a hair so the tongue is not too long, move the fence in to shave the tongue just outside the width of the groove, reverse for the second pass.

3 First test that the tongue fits the groove, then lower the blade and set the fence to cut the waste from the shoulders at the tongue's depth, fitting the joint as shown.

Tongue and Groove

The tongue is like an integral spline that reinforces and aligns the joint but takes a little more calculation to machine. Boards must be ripped wider to provide material for the tongue. Even without special groovers or a dado head, the tablesaw makes an acceptable joint with a combination or rip blade that has a raker, a square tooth that leaves the bottom of the kerf flat. Bowed lumber will misalign the groove or make the tongue uneven unless hold-downs and fingerboards are used to keep the lumber against the fence. Add a high wood fence for stability or to prevent cutters from contacting the metal fence.

The tongue and groove as a width joint is worth the extra trouble in production. Other times to use a tongue and groove: if the look at the end grain is preferred; in a dry assembly with a detailed edge like flooring; in a cabinet back; or in wainscotting, where exposure of the matching tongue from wood shrinkage is expected and tolerated. It also appears as a corner joint to assist carcass assembly, but the tongue is often offset.

Handplaned Rubbed Joint

Edge joints can be handplaned and glued without clamps by rubbing the tacky glue surfaces together. But rubbed joints can't be sprung, for without clamping, edge contact won't occur. Rubbing is suited to lengths under three feet, so a shooting board can be used for edge jointing. It requires glues that quickly develop tack such as animal glues or cross-linked aliphatics.

Shiplap

Each board of the shiplap must be wide enough to include the rabbet depth. Routed, shaped, or cut with a dado, the joint exposes additional long-grain gluing surface in a rabbet. It also serves to align the faces flush. In bowed lumber, this advantage is canceled unless there is downward clamping at the center of the boards, which is difficult to accomplish in a large slab glue-up.

Tongue and Bead

Adding a bead to the edge of a tongue-and-groove joint is a detail common to architectural finish work. Applied to assembled panels in furniture, such detailing of a tongue and groove adds visual interest and enables a dry-fitting option for handling wood movement over an expanse.

V-Groove

Edges without tongues can also be detailed, but such visual styling most often appears on vertical surfaces because of its tendency to catch debris. The V-groove or any similar detail accentuates the joint. It is easy to cut before glue-up but hard to keep free of glue squeeze-out.

Handplaned Rubbed Joint

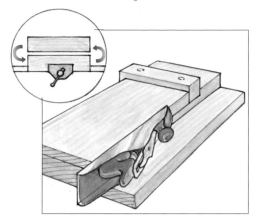

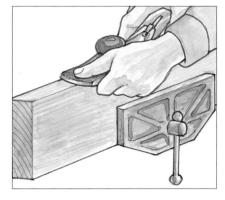

1 Shoot edges and test straightness, rotating one board against the other in the vise to find crowning that will rock the board or hollowing that causes the ends to scrape.

2 Check edges for squareness and correct any deviation by steadying the plane with a knuckle against the board and planing the high spot until a full shaving can be taken.

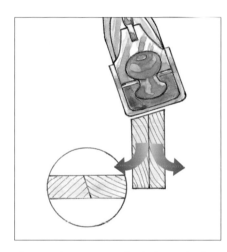

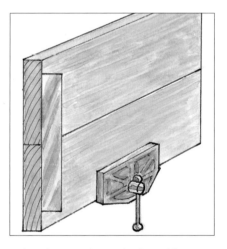

3 An alternative method planes both edges together in the vise so when aligned flat as shown, any deviation from 90 degrees is cancelled by the mating edge.

4 Whatever the method used for jointing the edges, a straightedge will lie flat across the joint if the technique is successful.

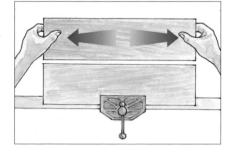

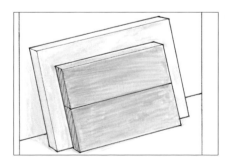

5 Lay thin stock flat for rubbing or clamp thicker stock in the vise, holding the top board low down to slide back and forth in the glue until suction grabs it.

6 Joints in thin wood shouldn't be disturbed until completely dry, but when it's safe to move the boards from the vise, lean them against a support until they dry thoroughly.

Shiplap

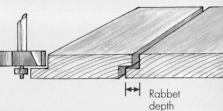

Rabbet depth

A shiplap is two mated rabbets that help alignment and increase the gluing surface but whose depth shouldn't be more than half the thickness of the stock.

Tongue and Bead

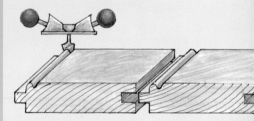

The tongue and bead, commonly seen in wainscoting, is a detail easily added to a tongue and groove with a router, molding plane, or scratch beader.

V-groove

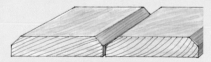

The tablesaw at 45 degrees or a plane or router can cut chamfers to form V-grooves for a paneling detail on the sides of a dresser or blanket chest.

About Scarf Joints

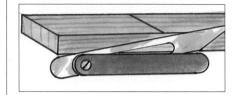

The shallow angle of the basic glued scarf (also called splice) exposes long-grain surfaces for a good glue joint. Simple gluing at the slope ratio of 1:8 bonds the parts into a unit that theory says is as strong as a single board. Like edge joints, there is no perfect solution to orienting the growth rings of solid wood scarfed parts – either to cup opposite to each other or to cup in the same direction. Worked scarfs that are more than simple glue joints also expose long grain for gluing, but in imitation of their timber-framing ancestors, begin to employ fitted joinery, locking, and pinning to hold the joint together. When scarfs are used structurally, another member should give direct or nearby support and, if needed, provide a place to hide a less than decorative joint. Used visually as a design element, elaborate scarf joints that defy machining are the most challenging and awe-inspiring of all woodworking joints.

A simple but effective scarf joint

1 Measure from each board end 8 times its thickness, square a line across the face, set the sliding bevel to the 1:8 angle and mark it on both edges.

2 If material size prevents wasting the acute bevel with any saw and planing smooth, start at the top corner and plane the entire bevel back to the squared line.

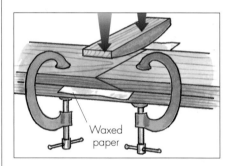
Waxed paper

3 Using waxed paper where glue may ooze, immobilize the parts against slipping and clamp the joint or, on a wide joint, use a crowned batten for pressure in the center.

End-to-End Scarf

Glue-scarfing boards end to end doesn't make a pretty joint, but for utility's sake, it's quite attractive. For extreme strength in a glue-only joint, use epoxy. With any glue, first spread a priming coat that will wick up into the grain, filling the hollow cells so the next coat stays at the gluing surface.

This scarf can be made angled, as it is used to angle a guitar's peg head back from the neck. In this application, both parts are aligned bevel side up, and one bevel is glued to the back of the other bevel, creating the angle. Draw the parts of a desired angle full-size in profile to find the angle setting for the sliding bevel to use in laying out the parts.

Edge-to-Edge Scarf

Scarfing edges oblique to the grain is also a utilitarian joint that joins lumber for length. It can be used to stretch out a too-short board by first ripping it diagonally, then sliding the halves a little along the cutting angle, gluing, and finally trimming to width when dry. A spline can reduce the extreme

angle required for a glue-only joint by introducing mechanical reinforcement and another gluing surface. Gluing is best preceded by a priming coat to prevent a glue-starved joint.

Squint-Butted Scarf

The squint-butted scarf is a simple start on worked scarfs. Resistant to bending, easy to reinforce and dress up with a transverse key, it has good long-grain contact for gluing. There is no set formula for the length of the lapping surface in worked scarfs. The joinery improves stress resistance or, in some designs, yields true parallel-grain gluing for strength instead of the oblique grain in glue-only joints. But scarf strength depends on the length of the scarf, so knowledge of the principles, an eye for aesthetics, and the application are the best guides. Regardless, layouts should be knife-scribed for exactness. Areas wasted with a saw should be cleaned up with a shoulder plane or chiseled down to the scribed line.

Edge-to-Edge Scarf

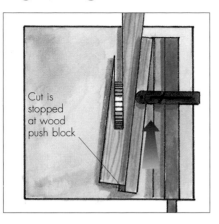

Cut is stopped at wood push block

1 For a strong glue joint, mark a taper 8 times the board's width, or set the jig to cut any angle under 20 degrees for non-structural work if the species glues well.

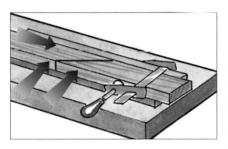

2 Apply glue and clamp one part to the fence of a non-stick gluing sled, press the mate in against it and clamp both to the fence until the joint dries.

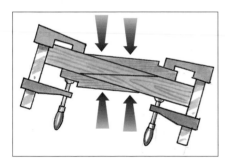

3 Alternatively, clamp the notched cutoffs to the parts, creating a parallel purchase for clamping the joint. Stop slipping by using a dowel, biscuit or headless brad pressed between the parts.

Squint-butted Scarf

1 Exactly scribe the edge's centerline 4 or more times as long as the board thickness. To this line's ends, scribe from each face parallel lines at 70 degrees.

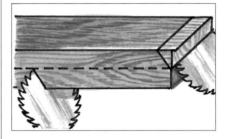

2 Set the saw blade to 70 degrees and cut both parts together if possible, using the miter gauge to trim the ends, then lower the blade and kerf the parts to the centerline.

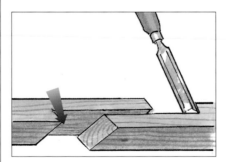

3 Use a handsaw, bandsaw, or tablesaw to cut the waste along the centerline, then guide a chisel against the shoulder to trim inside the corner and slide the joint together.

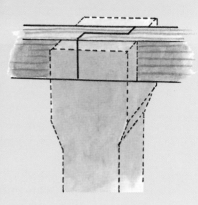

The unsightly joint line of a half-lapped or other light-duty scarf used to extend an apron can be supported and hidden inside a table leg.

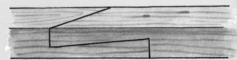

Angling the joining faces of any scarf increases resistance to tension and shear, but layout lines must be exactly scribed with a knife, sawn to, and shaved clean for a tight fit.

Angled ends resist bending, and inserting a transverse key into two aligning dadoes kerfed across a lowered sawblade additionally fortifies a joint against tension and shearing.

CHAPTER FOUR

LAPPED AND HOUSED JOINTS

ap joints are a simple family, suggesting their unique construction method, which reduces each part to half its thickness or width at the joint and laps one part over the other. They are also called "half-laps" or "halving joints". Laps appear in "L," "T," and crossed orientations. Housed joints use the same flat-bottomed milled elements as lap joints, but one part encloses or "houses" the other in an "L" or "T" orientation to serve some specific construction needs. Both these families can be modified.

About Lap Joints

The halving cuts that form lap joints are basically dadoes or rabbets, although wide dadoes are sometimes called trenches and deep dadoes are often termed notches. A halving cut in the board face results in a frame lap, used in supporting frameworks or more literally to frame panels. Edge laps notch into board edges to half the part's width and appear in crossed stretchers, sash moldings, shoji, chair back, or window lattice, and egg-crated dividers. The large gluing area of a frame lap is long-grain for a strong gluing but always with dimensional conflict. The edge lap has little long-grain contact and the wood is weakened by deep notching into the width and liable to split without reinforcement.

Rabbet
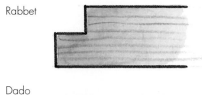

Dado

Notch
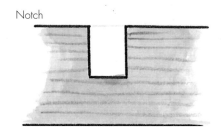

A lap joint in the T orientation is a simple combination of two basic elements.

The rabbet, the dado, and its deeper version, the notch, are the three basic cuts used to make halvings or lap joints.

That's why edge laps are light-duty joints or worked in plywood, whose alternated grains strengthen the material. Frame laps come in two basic versions: end laps are halving rabbets cut at the board's end; center laps are halving dadoes cut somewhere in the board's length (except at the very end or it loses a shoulder and becomes a rabbet). End laps and center laps (rabbets and dadoes) in different combinations form all the basic corner "L," "T," and crossed frame lap orientations.

Lap Joint Components

An end lap has a single shoulder and is formed by a deep rabbet cut to half the thickness of the stock.

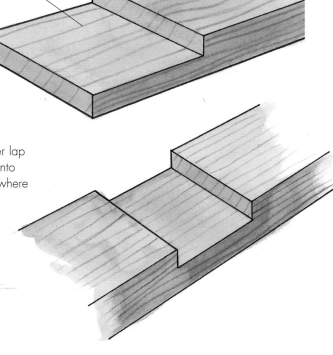

Shoulder

Cheek

A double-shouldered center lap has a dado or trench cut into the face of the board anywhere inside its length.

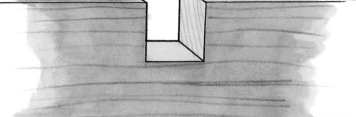

A deep dado notched into the edge of a board forms one half of an edge lap or edge halving joint.

Types of Lap Joint

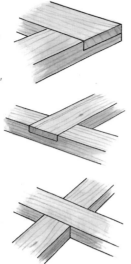

Halvings cut into the face of the board and assembled in "L," "T," or crossed configurations are called frame laps, with excellent gluing strength and shoulders that resist bending.

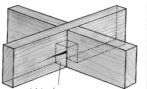

Weak area

A halving in the edge of the board is called an edge lap, but there is material weakness and no glue strength where unsupported end grain butts to the mating part.

Combining the Elements of Lap Joints

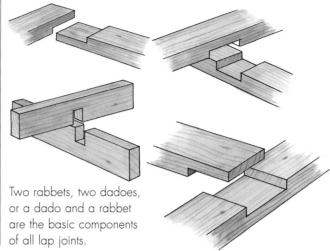

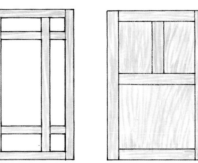

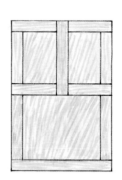

Two rabbets, two dadoes, or a dado and a rabbet are the basic components of all lap joints.

Using Lap Joints

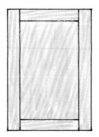

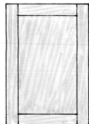

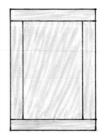

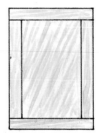

Straight and angled laps are good joints for decorative lattice work in windows, doors, outdoor furniture, and structures like gazebos.

It's possible to join a traditional-style door entirely with lap joints that are nearly as strong as mortise and tenon, but the front and back won't have the same visual lines.

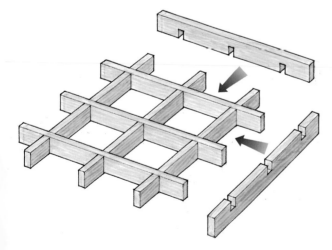

Make egg-crate dividers on the tablesaw with a notching jig, or saw down by hand and chop out the waste at the bottom of the cut with a chisel.

On doors where one side is prominent, lap different pairs of parts on top to shift the design emphasis from a vertical to a horizontal line.

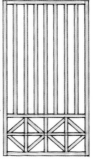

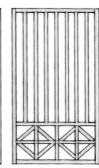

The latticework of Japanese shoji screens is joined by straight and angled lap joints, usually sawn simultaneously in soft wood by hand while the mating parts are clamped together.

Shopmade Aids to Making Lap Joints

Jigs for Handheld Tools

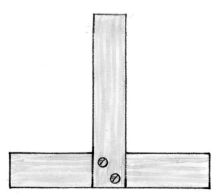

A smooth, straight edge to guide tools squarely across the workpiece is a basic shop accessory that is especially useful when making lap joints.

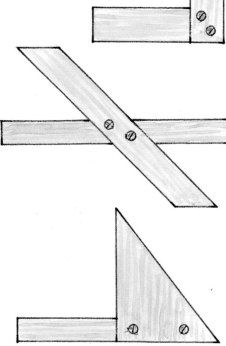

Angled fences to guide cuts by router, plane, or saw are cheap and easy to make using a protractor head, T-bevel, or full-sized shop drawing in order to set the angle.

Routing Methods

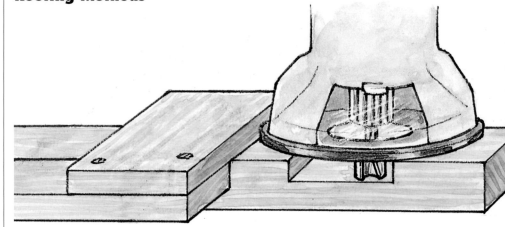

A shopmade square fence guides a router base to make an end lap while excess end material helps to support the router and is cut off later.

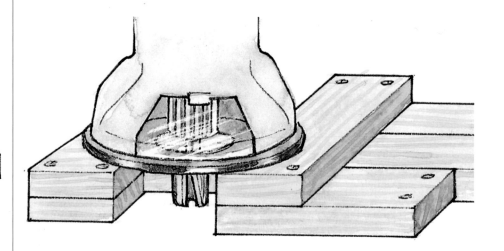

To rout multiples, the workpiece slides under a fence that guides an over-bearing straight bit and is stopped at the shoulder mark by a block that also supports the router.

Jigs for Tablesaws and Router Tables

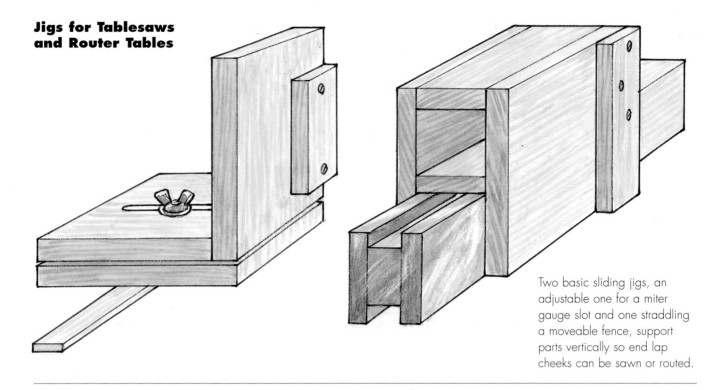

Two basic sliding jigs, an adjustable one for a miter gauge slot and one straddling a moveable fence, support parts vertically so end lap cheeks can be sawn or routed.

Jigs for Miter Gauge

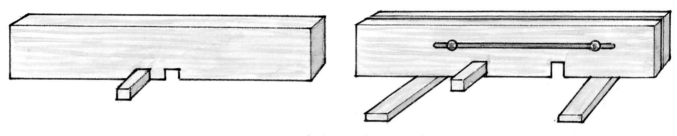

Two jigs assist repetition of edge notches: one rides miter gauge slots and has an adjustable fence, the other attaches to the miter gauge. (See Box Joint on the Tablesaw on page 58.)

Gluing Lap Joints

For a good glue bond, always use a block under the clamp head to distribute pressure so the long-grain surfaces make full contact.

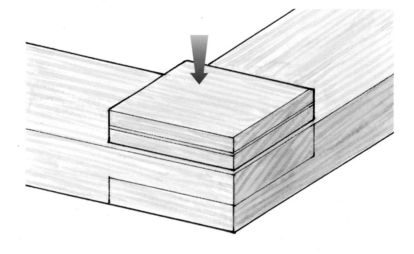

End Laps

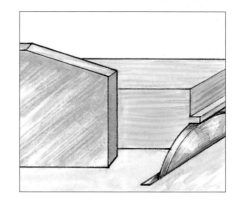

One end lap can combine with another end lap to form an L-corner lap or it can set into a center lap to make a T-lap joint. Put together in an I-formation, an end lap becomes a scarf joint, covered in Chapter 3 (see pages 44–45). There are always more ways to machine joints than are shown here, and the techniques for sawing cheeks and shoulders by hand are included in the chapter on Mortise and Tenon Joints (see pages 76–77).

1 Graze a scrap end of the stock with a lowered sawblade, flipping the stock each subsequent cut and slowly raising the blade until it removes the lip at the center.

One of the safest methods to align a cut is by clamping a spacer block to the saw fence in front of the blade (as shown with the tablesawn end lap). The part should clear the block before the cut is completed, and better, before it starts. It's a hazardous practice to use the fence and miter gauge together to make repetitive cut-offs because the cut part can bind between the fence and blade and be thrown back. Some feel that when parts are only kerfed or dadoed and not cut off, it's safe to use the miter gauge and fence together. Using a spacer block *any* time these two are used in tandem ensures it.

Cheeks and shoulders can be cut by router whether most of the material is wasted by sawing as shown, or wasted completely by routing. A router table is a handy assistant, but routing the parts handheld (as shown in Center Lap on pages 54–55) is also a good solution. If many parts are needed, set up a jig to assist in repetitive cutting and to avoid tedious clamping and unclamping of fences. Several jigs are shown on the previous page.

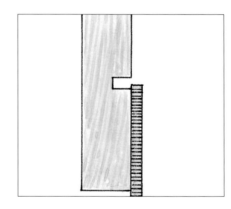

4 After the shoulders are cut on all the parts, raise the blade height into the kerf but not so it nicks the new shoulder.

End Lap Variations

Some ways to mechanically reinforce corner lap joints are shown here, or to use a lap joint to add gluing strength to the always weak end grain miter. But because of their substantial long-grain gluing surface, unless they need to resist considerable tension, just gluing laps is usually strong enough.

Bandsawn and Routed End Lap

1 Square a shoulder line at stock width, mark an edge centerline, kerf into the waste near the shoulder and set a stop block at cutting depth to waste the cheek.

2 Fit the router table with a straight bit and bump-cut the edge of some scrap stock, then flip and cut again, raising the bit until the cuts center.

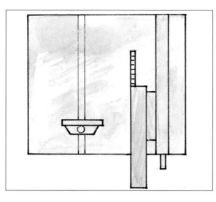

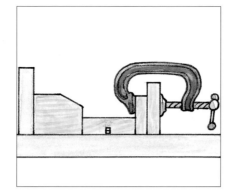

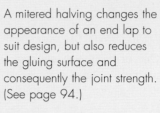

2 Place the stock and a scrap block against the fence and slide the entire assembly over until the edge of the stock aligns with the outer tooth of the blade.

3 Lock the fence and clamp the scrap to it in front of the blade, then butt the stock against the block and push the cut through with the miter gauge.

A mitered halving changes the appearance of an end lap to suit design, but also reduces the gluing surface and consequently the joint strength. (See page 94.)

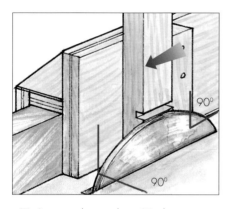

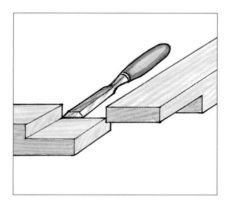

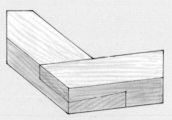

5 Support the stock at 90 degrees to the table and move the fence in until the blade aligns to the depth of the shoulder kerf and clears any screws.

6 After wasting the cheeks using the jig, clean up the inside corner with a chisel if the blade leaves a tiny ridge there, and assemble the joint.

Tilt the sawblade slightly and stop-cut one cheek end first, shaving the other part's cheek held upright to fortify a weight-bearing framing lap, like one for a glass door.

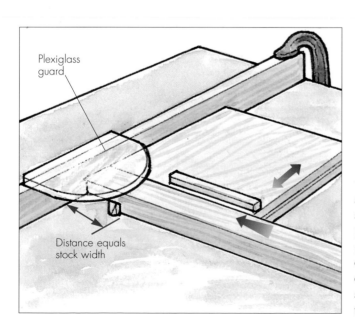

Plexiglass guard

Distance equals stock width

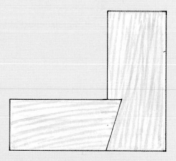

3 With a square of grip-cleated scrap plywood to steady it, clean the joint by feeding the part back and forth across the bit while at the same time sliding it toward the fence-stop.

Halve a single dovetail and scribe its angled shoulder on the back of the mating part as another way to reinforce against tension on the glue line. (See page 105.)

Center Lap

There are many methods for removing the waste between the shoulders of a center lap. Sawing repetitive kerfs to half the part's thickness, either by hand or machine, weakens the material so it can be broken out and the cheek cleaned up by chiseling, hand planing, or routing. Another way is to rout out the cheek material with a handheld router as shown below, or remove it using a router table aided by a miter gauge or sliding jig to steady the part. A technique for centering a router bit in the stock is shown in Bandsawn and Routed End Lap on page 52.

Possibly no other joint requires so much material removal as a halving joint. A dado head cutter removes material quite effectively, but some types of dado heads don't leave an entirely flat bottom, or the outer teeth leave deeper scribe marks with each cut that will show at the glue line. With heads like this, wasting cuts have to be held short of the centerline and cleaned up by hand tools or router.

A project that requires tedious cutting of numerous duplicates will become the mother of invention. A saddle jig, shown in Shopmade Aids to Making Lap Joints, can be modified so the sides that guide the router are spaced farther apart. The router then has to travel side to side as well as forward and back. The side-to-side play can be calculated to stop at the same distance apart as the center lap shoulders, saving time setting fences and measuring.

Another way to make multiples is to cut one halving across a wide board and rip the board into the narrower parts required. The only drawback is that this method gives less flexibility to choose what grain will show in the finished piece than there is when parts are milled individually, and there are two faces and two different edges up to choose.

Center Lap by Hand

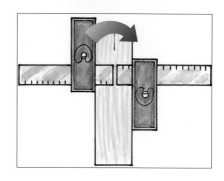

1 Scribe a line near the end grain's center, flip the square and scribe again, split the marks and set the blade to the exact center, then scribe the end and joint's edge.

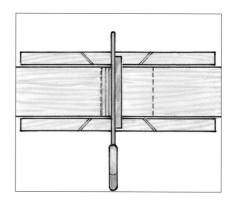

4 Lay out the shoulders as far apart as the width of the stock to be joined, and square them across to make a series of saw cuts between them in the waste.

Routed Center Lap

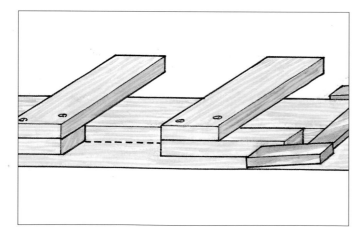

1 Scribe the joint's centerline and shoulders, align some square shopmade router guides across the stock on the shoulder lines, and clamp them there.

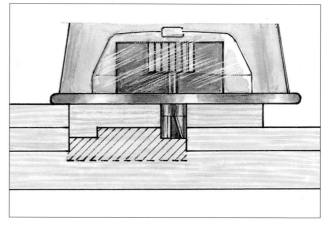

2 Guiding a router and top-bearing straight bit from left to right against the jigs, make shallow passes that cut the shoulders, then waste the material between them.

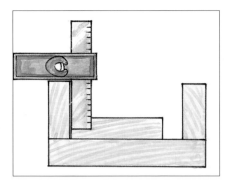

2 Put the stock, blocked up if
necessary, in a miter box and extend
and lock the square's blade just shy of
the center mark on the end of the stock.

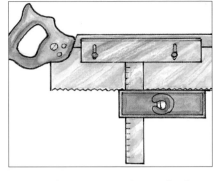

3 Use the setting to adjust a depth
stop on the saw, covering the
square's beam temporarily with masking
tape or taking care not to scrape the
saw's teeth on it.

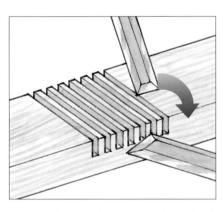

5 Break away the waste with a chisel
and carefully pare the ridges that
will be left at the bottom of the joint plus
any saw marks on the shoulders.

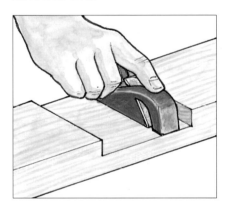

6 If possible, use a bullnose, shoulder,
or rabbet plane in order to square
the shoulders and flatten the bottom level
with the edge centerline for the best
glue surface.

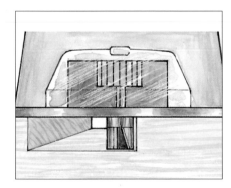

3 If a short bit can't reach the
centerline, remove the jigs and use
the new shoulders as guides for the
bearing, continuing shallow passes to
reach the joint's bottom.

Center Lap Variations

A fully housed center lap is often a
face-frame joint for built-ins where
the end grain won't show, or just a
stabilizing rail. But without a shoulder
on the housed part, the rack resistance
isn't as good as with two halved and
shouldered parts. A joint that is halved
and lapped with a dovetailed end like
the dovetailed center or T-lap has high
tension and rack resistance and is an
excellent contributor to solid framed
structures. The cogged lap has
internal rack resistance that is easier
to hide if joinery isn't a design
feature. It also would be useful as a
stabilizing center stile in a structure
like shelving with lipped edges.

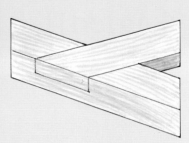

A full lap houses one part's
thickness in another part's face;
a face housing sets the full part
into an edge, making joints
especially useful when the thinner
part continues past.

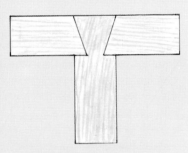

Cut a single or double dovetail
on an end lap and scribe
around it to mark the center lap
shoulders for strengthening a
T-lap against tension. (See
Dovetail Joints on page 105.)

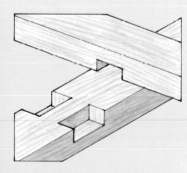

A crossing joint without a family,
a cogged part lapped by a
halving has excellent resistance
to racking if flush faces aren't
required and chiseling time-
consuming sockets is tolerable.

Angled T-Lap and Jigged Edge Lap

Angled T-Lap

It's very easy to cut the angle of the center lap tilted in the wrong direction if careful attention isn't paid to laying it out for final assembly. The radial-arm saw is only one method for milling this joint. It's simple to rout handheld using an angled fence. The tablesaw also will cut the cheeks of the T-part, aided by a sliding fence jig like that shown in End Lap on the Tablesaw on pages 52–53. Since the T-ends aren't square but angled, the support block on the jig has to be tilted away from the blade to the angle that holds the end of the mitered T-part flat against the table.

Use the tablesaw miter gauge to steady the work for repeated kerfs across the center lap to waste the material between the shoulders. A dadoing head will waste the center lap material, but watch out for it lifting the part off the table.

Jigged Edge Lap

The edge notching jig is useful if a number of notches and parts are being cut. For one or two joints, handsawing in a miter box, like the technique shown in Full Housing by Hand (see page 62), then chopping out the waste with a chisel is a lot quicker.

The jig works on the tablesaw or router table, but with either machine, tear-out at the back of the workpiece where the cutter passes through is more than difficult to control, especially in soft or coarse-grained woods. A scrap backing board between the workpiece and fence will help, or cut all the notches to width in over-thick stock and make clean-up passes by handplane, planer, or saw in order to thickness the parts to fit the notches. Milling notches across one wide, thick board and ripping notched strips from it is another option against tear-out. So is taking the opportunity to test Japanese handtools and techniques by clamping all the parts together to handsaw simultaneously and chisel out the waste.

1 Mark the angled shoulder position on the faces of the parts, squaring it around to the back of the center-lap part and scribing it by using the bevel gauge setting.

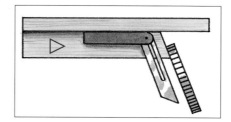

2 Use the same angle to set the radial-arm sawblade and cut the end lap part to length.

Jigged Edge Lap

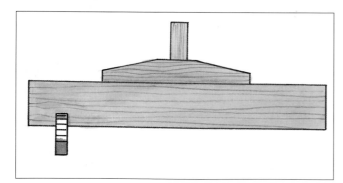

1 Match the stock thickness to a router bit or dado cutter mounted in a tablesaw and use a miter gauge to notch a scrap ½ the stock width deep.

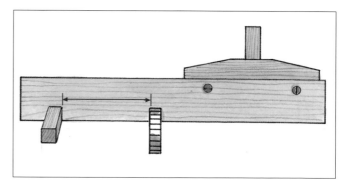

2 Fit an indexing key to the notch, clamp the scrap to the miter gauge, cut a second notch at the desired spacing, screw the scrap to the gauge and unclamp.

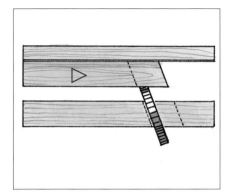

3 Raise the blade to the centerline of the stock thickness and kerf across at the shoulder lines, then waste the center lap material with a series of kerfs across it.

4 Turn the blade to the horizontal position and clamp a height table for clearance to the saw fence, then mark the cutting path of the blade's outer diameter on it.

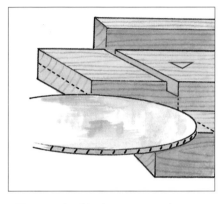

5 Raise the blade to cut into the cheek waste at the centerline and pull the cut through, taking care that the part's shoulder doesn't move beyond the marked blade path.

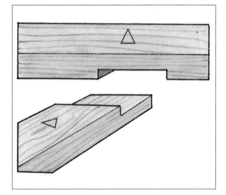

6 Clean up the cheeks with a chisel or shoulder plane if necessary, turn the center-lapped part face up and assemble the joint.

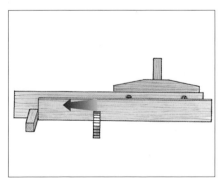

3 Butt the stock to the index key to cut the first notch, then fit the notch over the index and cut again, advancing the stock for each new notch.

Angled and Edge Lap Variations

The simplest way to find the angles for an angled cross lap is to draw a square on paper, or start from a corner of a sheet of plywood to lay out the actual height and width of the "X" and take the crossing angles from it with an architect's triangle or T-bevel. Pin through the joint with dowels or plugged screws for extra reinforcement as there's nowhere to add another shoulder like the edge halving bridle joint. Another way to add strength is to increase the shoulder proportion as in the shouldered angled lap.

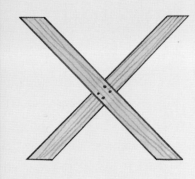

The angled cross lap, reinforceable with pins, gives good support to casual tables while the angled edge lap allows stretchers between table and chairs legs to run diagonally.

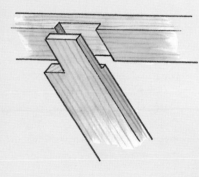

Decreasing the width of the angled lap strengthens the center lap member by removing less wood while proportionately fortifying the shoulder base against racking.

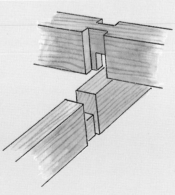

Reinforcing an edge lap against twisting by housing the thickness of one member in secondary dadoes marries the edge lap to the bridle joint family. (See Mortise and Tenon Joints on page 69.)

Box Joint on the Tablesaw

The box joint, also called the fingerlap joint, is a design spawned by machinery. It's possible to cut it by hand, but this is one case where humans are imitating machines. Aesthetically, the proportions of fingers and notches look best if they are as wide as the stock thickness, half the stock thickness, or the thickness of a sawblade kerf. This last joint is also referred to as a comb joint. If a friction fit is achieved, the exceptional amount of long-grain glue surface between the fingers makes the fingerlap the dovetail's rival for strength.

As with the edge lap and its jig, machining the box joint on the tablesaw presents the problem of tear-out. The box joint notch parallels the grain instead of crossing it as it does in the edge lap, so the tear-out is only at the top of the notch, not at both sides. Scribing a line across the board where the top will fall is the method shown to control tear-out. One scribed line will show on each face because the technique allows for designs that won't always accommodate an exact number of fingers and notches on the part, like drawers fit to a space. It makes any pattern deviations fall at the bottom edge. The scribed line can be planed off, left to show as in the dovetail layouts on antique furniture, or balanced by adding a line. The alternative method, using a scrap backer board behind the part, is helpful but not foolproof.

Routing a box joint on a router table with the jig is most successful in thin stock. The thicker the stock, the deeper the notch, and the amount of material becomes too much for the router bit to take off in one pass. An up-shear, carbide spiral cutter might work better than a regular fluted bit, or else use a high-speed steel aluminum-cutting end mill with a high cutting angle and good chip clearance for the larger wood chip.

Making a Box Joint on the Tablesaw

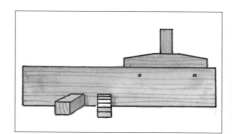

1 Make a jig for the miter gauge like the edge lap jig, but match the key, notch, and spacing to the dado's width, and set the notch height just under the stock thickness.

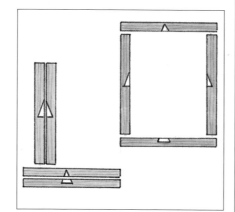

2 Choose the outside faces and mark the parts to distinguish sides from fronts and backs, and to show the reference edge to be used against the indexing key.

3 With the reference edge close and the end always at the left hand, scribe across each end at a setting just over the stock thickness to minimize tear-out.

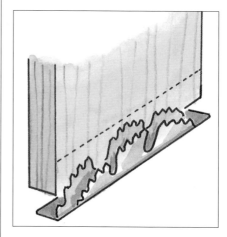

4 Set the dado height to the scribed line to leave the fingers proud for sanding flush after assembly, a practice anticipated at the start by cutting stock slightly over final length.

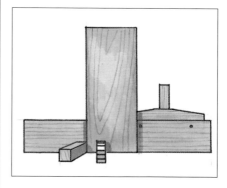

5 Butt a side's reference edge against the key with scribed face toward the jig, cut a notch, then check that the new notch and finger are exactly the same width.

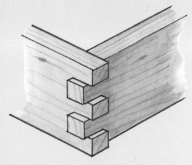

Cutting notches deeper than the stock thickness lets the fingers of a box joint stand proud for a decorative effect that is additionally enhanced by chamfering around each finger's end.

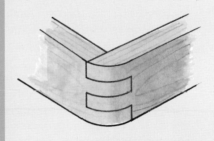

After a box joint is glued, round the corner by hand or with a router for a bricklaid appearance that is friendly to the touch.

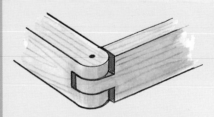

Dry-assemble the fingers and drill through their centers, round the ends, and then insert a waxed dowel or brass pin to make a wood hinge for joining to a box lid.

6 Reverse the side and index it over the key, then butt a front or back against it with the scribed line in to cut a notch at its reference edge.

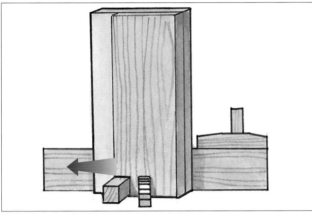

7 To gang the dadoing, turn the side back around and index it over the key, butt up the back's half notch, and advance the parts together to cut additional notches.

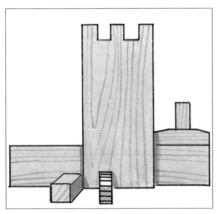

8 Keeping the reference edges toward the key, turn the boards end for end and repeat, making sure to start each part with a finger or notch like its other end.

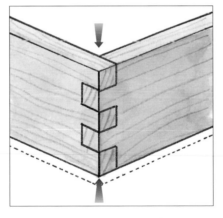

9 Trim any bottom waste edge to width so a wider or narrower last finger will fall there and glue together so clamping pressure seats the fingers and enhances long-grain contact.

Box Joint Variations

The decorative effect of box joints is a starting point for alterations and applications that draw attention to the interlocking pattern of the fingers. One famous woodworker has used the hinging option to attach drop-leaves at the ends of his tabletops. He staggers the ends of the glued-up boards in the top to create fingers and notches, then fits in and pins an alternately staggered leaf.

Housed Joints

Although they are made from the same basic cuts as lap joints, instead of the equal partnership of lap joints, housed joints have an implied hierarchy because one part *houses* the other. In joint terminology, there's a difference between the hous*er* and the hous*ee*. When a cabinet back is set into a rabbet, the joint is called a rabbet housing. If the rabbet itself is housed, it's a housed rabbet. But the basic housing cut (the houser) is always a dado, rabbet, or groove.

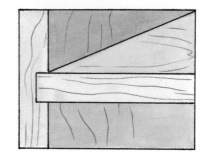

A full dado housing encloses the thickness of the joining part and both parts move as a unit across their widths, but all the glue surface is end grain.

A joint is a full housing when it fully encloses one part (the housee) in the U-shape of a dado or groove, or the "step" of a rabbet. A partial housing encloses some of the part, usually a tongue, while one or two shoulders bear on the face of the wood that the housing is cut in to stabilize the joint. But even if shoulders improve on the full housing's lack of racking resistance, housed joints are not very strong. Aside from having no mechanical resistance to tension unless they are modified, in most "T" orientations with dado housings like shelving and some "L" orientations with rabbet housings, there is no long-grain contact for gluing. But the shear resistance of the joint used for shelving is suited to the purpose, and a cabinet back adds the needed stability.

Dovetails are used to modify the tongues of housed parts and the housings themselves to increase tension resistance in housed joints. Housed, sliding, and other varieties of dovetails are covered in the chapter on Dovetail Joints (see pages 104-115). Other methods of increasing tension resistance usually involve putting screws into the tongue of a T-joint or driving fasteners diagonally through it, practices that suggest a lesser quality of crafting. Thoughtful design of the overall structure and the housed joints within it, or even a special glue like epoxy, make fasteners unnecessary.

The most common housed joints are the ones used to join fixed shelving into place, but housings also hold drawer runners and drawer frames inside carcasses, let cabinet backs be set in, or like the pinned rabbet housing shown in Full-housed Variations, page 63 serve as the popular drawer corner joint of Japanese woodworking. Housings modified by dovetails mechanically prevent racking or correct bowing as cross-members in framed structures like table aprons, and as shelf joints resist forces pushing tall cabinet sides outward.

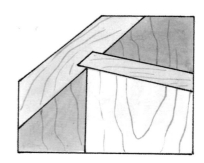

A full grooved housing runs with the grain, and the housed part's grain is best run parallel so there is no dimensional conflict and the glue bond is excellent.

Shopmade Aids to Making Housed Joints

A T-square fence guides dadoes by a router if it's run along the fence into the beam, cutting the dado width and location to align the fence and layout.

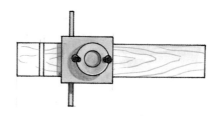

An auxiliary router base with a fixed runner that matches the cutter's width and is set the dado's spacing from it will cut equidistant dadoes, each cut aligning the next.

Attach a depth stop through holes drilled slowly into a tenon saw to avoid losing blade temper, or use small spring or C-clamps to hold the stop on.

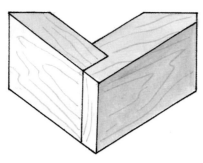

As a corner joint, a full rabbet housing has no glue strength and no resistance to tension unless it's reinforced.

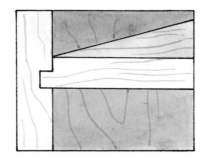

A shoulder increases racking resistance in a partial housing, also called a housed rabbet, but there is still no resistance to tension, even though shear strength remains high.

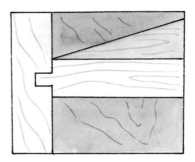

Two shoulders in a partial housing might increase rack resistance but they aren't worth the possible reduced shear strength.

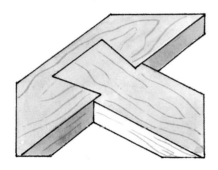

Increasing tension resistance in a full housing means using elements from other joint families to create a suitable joint, in this case a full housed lap dovetail.

A stopped housing is held short of the part's edge and the joining member, in this case a shelf, is notched back slightly at the face to hide the joinery.

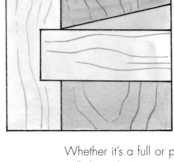

Whether it's a full or partial housing, a through housing will show the intersection of the parts at the face.

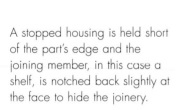

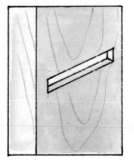

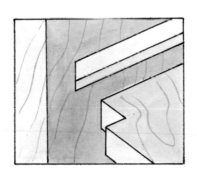

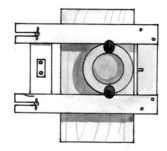

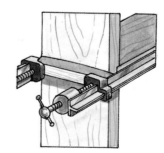

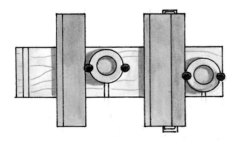

Another fence, shown in Routed Housed Rabbet on pages 64–65, will space equidistant dadoes by router, but an additional spacer strip can be added in to increase the height between shelves.

A saddle jig fits over the workpiece and the sides guide the router across it from the end entry hole to cut through or be stopped by a block.

In order to transfer clamp pressure to the center of long dadoes, cut slightly crowned cauls for each shelf end and tighten a bar clamp parallel to each edge of the shelf.

Full Housing

A full housing has little resistance to racking and less to tension, so the overall structure has to be considered before this joint is chosen. A tapped-home fit makes the joint work mechanically and aesthetically, but it is a fit that is easily lost to sanding of the housed part. With no shoulder to cover any deviations along the dado edge, accuracy and the flatness of the housed part are both in sharp focus.

A housing deeper than half the thickness of the part will weaken it: A depth one third the thickness is all that's necessary. If housing drawer runners in solid wood so crossgrain construction is introduced, screw the runners at the front of the carcass and slot-screw them at the back without glue to allow for wood movement. Make runners or drawer frames a little short of the back or shrinkage of the sides will cause these long-grained parts to push on it. Runners or drawer frames in plywood housings can be glued.

Full-Housed Variations

Increasing the full housing's resistance to tension isn't hard, but frequently it means borrowing from the dovetail family. Full dovetail housings have their own difficulties (covered in the chapter on Dovetail Joints, see page 103), but the joint shown is a quick and easy strengthening modification. At the front few inches of the dado, the dado's square U-shape is stopped and a narrower dovetail housing is cut. A short section of the shelf end is shaped to match, and the joint slides home from the back. For more on sliding dovetails, see page 112.

If the grain of the parts run vertically, a full rabbet housing makes a strong glue joint. But like other full housings, a full rabbet housing at a corner with only end grain contact won't hold together under tension unless it's reinforced. Pinning is one good cure that makes a quick but strong drawer corner joint.

Full Housing by Hand

1 Mark one shoulder of each dado on the board's face, planning waste to fall on the same side of the marks, then transfer the layout to mating parts.

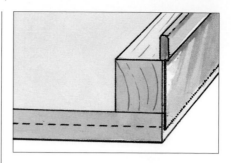

2 Cut a block whose height added to the dado depth will equal the sawblade measured from teeth to back.

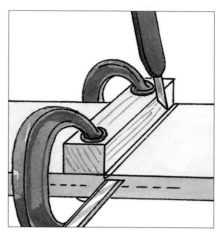

3 Clamp the block square across the stock at the mark, score the board along the block, then chisel a small bevel in the waste side to guide the saw.

Stopped Full Housing on the Tablesaw

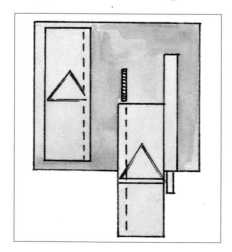

1 Mark the dado parts for reassembly and rip and save narrow strips from their front edges so each part equals the desired width when the strips are reglued later.

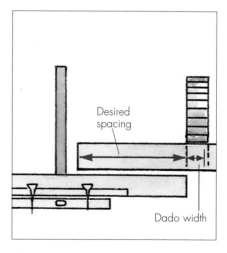

2 Screw a scrap fence to the miter gauge and trim its end with a dado cutter matched to shelf thickness, then dado another scrap at the desired depth and spacing.

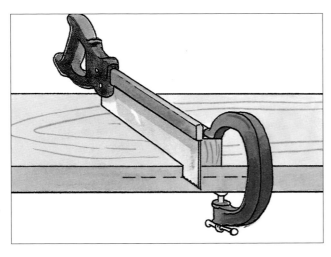

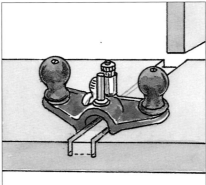

4 Guiding the saw against the block and into the chiseled bevel, cut across the board until the saw reaches the dado depth when its back hits the stop block.

5 With the block still clamped in place, use the thickness of the stock to be housed as a gauge to score a line for the other shoulder of the dado.

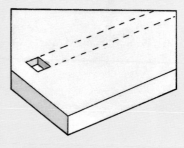

6 Align the block on the second score and repeat the sawing process, then chisel or router plane to a flat bottom at the desired depth and fit the shelf.

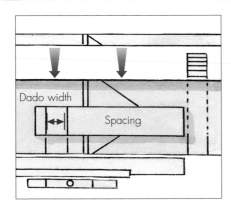

3 Lay out dadoes using the spacing scrap, aligning marks to the scrap fence's end to cut each dado; when done cutting, reglue the edge strip, notching the shelf front to fit around it.

Full Housing on the Tablesaw

For aesthetic reasons, the housing is sometimes stopped back from the front edge. The front corner of the shelf that would be housed in a through dado is cut off, notching in a small shoulder that bears on the material left in front of the dado by stopping it. A stopped cut on a tablesaw is difficult and dangerous, especially one running crossgrain, and the stopped kerf of the blade leaves an arc to square up. Removing a thin strip from the front edge before dadoing and regluing it later resolves the mechanical and aesthetic problems of dadoing on the tablesaw.

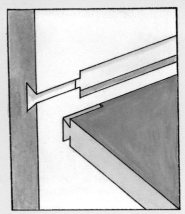

A short dovetailed section at the front of a full housing strengthens the joint against tension but avoids the problems of a full sliding dovetail (see Sliding Dovetails, page 112).

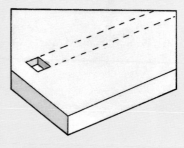

To make a stopped dado by hand, first drill a flat-bottomed hole to dado depth at the front, squaring it with a chisel to make traveling room for the saw.

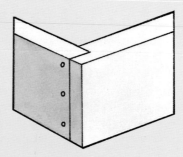

The rabbet housing is a simple corner joint that has no glue strength, but reinforced with pins is strong enough for drawer fronts or other corners where visible end grain is acceptable.

Housed Rabbet Joints

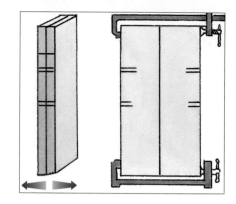

One shoulder added to a housing joint improves the racking resistance and resolves the problems of fitting a full housing for a clean look. Two shoulders weaken the housed part unnecessarily.

For shelving, the housed rabbet is superior to the full housing, but the full housing is a better choice for interior carcass mechanicals like drawer runners. Milled as housed rabbets, they lack the material for milling the screw slots needed to attach them. For a cleaner look when housing these parts, cut a tiny cosmetic shoulder just to cover the joinery line. Drawer frames can use either joint.

1 Choose a straight bit diameter ½ to ⅔ the shelf thickness, next lay out two dadoes and spacing on mated uprights, and then clamp open and square the marks around.

Routed and Stop-Routed Housed Rabbet

The method shown allows cutting a full housed rabbet with one straight bit for dadoing and no router fence accessory or any additional rabbeting bit to cut the rabbet. Either of these would eliminate the fence and gauge used to space it from the shelf ends to cut the rabbets with a straight bit. The gauge is faster and more accurate than measuring for fence placement if many shelves are involved.

The beauty of through housings is their faster fabrication; the drawback is the joinery showing. A housed rabbet cut through isn't particularly pretty at the front edge of a structure. A face frame will cover it, but it takes additional time to make. Thus, the choice between a through housing or the "slower" stopped housing becomes a matter of design.

Aligning the cut to the layout and stopping the dado with a saddle jig is convenient. The jig better controls staying on the line and stopping at the right spot; it improves accuracy and reduces the stress of working.

Housed Rabbet Variations

Again the dovetail comes to the rescue of the housed joint against the forces of tension. A half or single-shouldered dovetail is the easiest housed dovetail to make, but since it slides in from the back, it's sometimes difficult to get the parts in over a long dado when they swell with glue (see the chapter on Dovetail Joints, page 112).

Housing a rabbet at a board's end for certain corner joints is one place where the housed joint replaces dovetails. Although the joint isn't as strong as dovetails overall, placed in tension at a cabinet bottom or drawer corner, the housed rabbet is a serviceable joint if the short grain is sufficient and the drawer bottom or cabinet back reduces racking. It's close cousin, the tongue and lap, improves on the problem of a corner housed rabbet's visible end grain.

4 Guide the router against the fence to run the second dado, advancing the fence to each new dado to space successive cuts with the fence clamped in place if necessary.

Stop-Routed Housed Rabbet

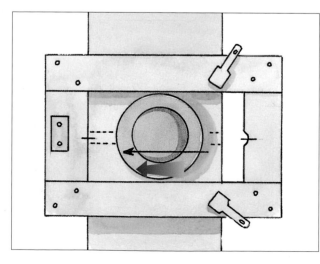

1 Align the saddle jig centerline to the dado centerline and set a block to stop the router just short of the front edge of the dado stock.

2 Measure from bit to sub-base edge and offset a fence this distance from the dado layout, cutting the first dado between the marks about ⅓ the thickness in depth.

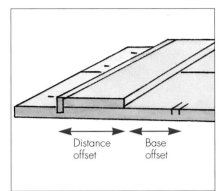

3 Fit a runner snugly into the dado, then measure from it to the next dado, subtract the base offset, rip a fence to this width and attach it to the runner.

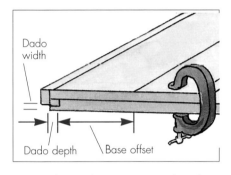

5 Make another gauge equaling the base offset plus the dado depth and use it to set a fence for rabbeting tongues on the shelf ends that fit the dado's width.

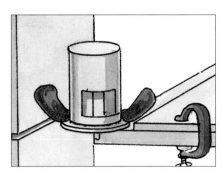

6 Cut rabbets on each shelf end so the distance between shelf shoulders equals the desired dimension between uprights and the tongues aren't too long to keep shoulders from seating.

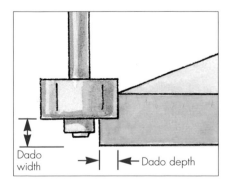

2 Cut the rabbets with a rabbeting bit whose cutting depth equals the dado depth and rout down until the tongue thickness fits the dado width snugly.

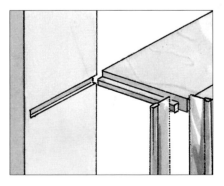

3 Saw away a length of the tongue to match the set-back of the stopped dado, pare the shoulder there, and test that the front edges of the joint align flush.

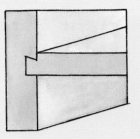

When outward forces are expected (like the weight of leaning books on a tall case), a half dovetail tongue reinforces the joint against tension (see Dovetail Joints, page 112).

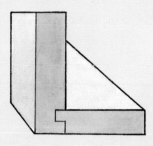

The housed rabbet joins cabinet tops and bottoms to the sides and drawer backs and fronts to their sides if drawer-front end grain will be covered by an attached face.

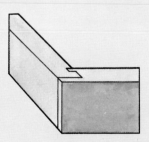

A tongue and lap, made from an end grain dado with one side cut short for the tongue, combines joint families to prevent end grain showing on a drawer front.

CHAPTER FIVE

MORTISE AND TENON

The mortise and tenon joint has been an effective method for joining wood at right angles since ancient times. Its basic form and variations continue to serve as a primary method for joining frames, leg assemblies, and carcass skeletons.

A tenon is a long tongue that fits into a pocket, or mortise, in a mating part. Like lap joints, the mortise and tenon are glued cheek to cheek, but unlike lap joints where one long-grain cheek is glued to the other, the mortise and tenon doubles the gluing surface by bonding two tenon face cheeks to two long-grain mortise cheeks. Also like lap joints, the cheeks are glued crossgrain, so some dimensional conflict is inherent in mortise and tenon joints as it is in laps.

About the Mortise and Tenon

There are two basic tenon types that mate with two basic mortise types. A through tenon fits into a through mortise, a hole right through the mortised part. A stub or blind tenon fits into a blind mortise, one which bottoms in the material of the mortised part instead of passing through it. Mortise shapes are mostly rectilinear, round, or a long slot with rounded ends.

The shoulders that are added to the tenon serve several purposes. They increase rack resistance to stabilize the joint. They move the tenon (and with it the mortise) away from the weaker ends or edges of mortised parts. They cover the joint's edges and create a depth stop. Both tenon shoulders and mortises can be angled to modify the basic T or L square orientation of the mortise and tenon.

A family of joints called bridle joints, the relatives between lap joints and the mortise and tenon, is included here. Bridle joints are also called slip joints, slot mortises, or open slot mortises, which is descriptive of their assembly method where one part bridles or "slips" over another part. Their specialized mortise is always cut into end grain.

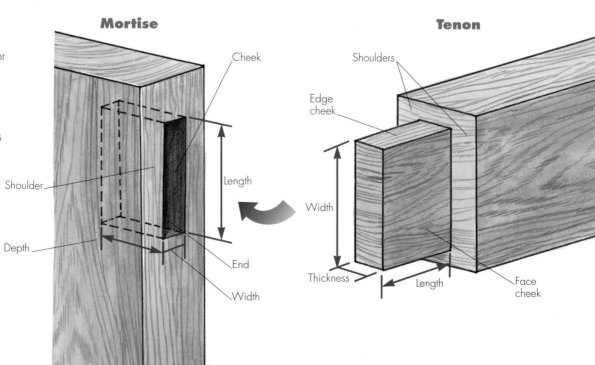

An open slot mortise is a relative of the mortise and tenon.

The Basic Types of Mortise

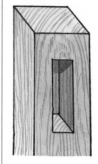

A blind mortise has a flat bottom that stops short of the opposite face, and the tenon end is enclosed by the wood.

A through mortise makes a hole through the material, and once the joint is assembled, the tenon end can be seen on the other side.

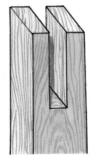

The specialized slot mortise is nothing more than a deep dado cut in the end of the part and used in slip or bridle joints, mortise and tenon relatives.

Mortise and Tenon Terminology

The pocket of the mortise accepts a projecting tongue or tenon and is an age-old method for joining wood parts of the same or different thicknesses at right angles.

Mortise

Cheek

Shoulder

Depth

Length

End

Width

Tenon

Shoulders

Edge cheek

Width

Thickness

Length

Face cheek

The Basic Types of Tenon

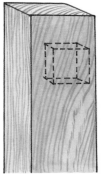

A blind or stub tenon is enclosed by a blind mortise and doesn't pass through the mortised part.

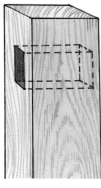

A through tenon inserted in a through mortise extends at least to the opposite face of the mortised part and sometimes beyond it.

The Basic Types of Tenon Shoulders

A tenon is barefaced when there are no shoulders on the face sides, which directs its use to slats or thin material that would be weakened by shoulders.

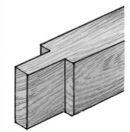

Tenons with two front shoulders are the perfect mate for a slot mortise, but in through or blind mortises they lack edge shoulders to hide over-long or marred mortise ends.

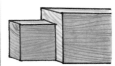

Cutting one or two edge shoulders on a barefaced tenon increases the rack resistance of the joint, sets an exact length on the part, and creates a positive depth stop.

A third shoulder moves a tenon and its mating mortise away from a frame corner so both mortise and tenon are enclosed by wood in the joint.

A single front shoulder makes a tenon resemble an end lap and offsets it for certain applications, but the tenon is still considered barefaced.

Four shoulders are difficult to align around the entire part and are often unnecessary except when the joint will be carved or shaped after assembly.

The Evolution of Joint Families

In the corner L orientation, it's easy to see the evolution of joint families from end laps to slot mortises to mortise and tenon joints.

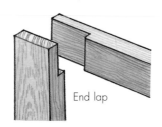

End lap

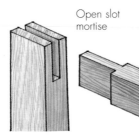

Open slot mortise

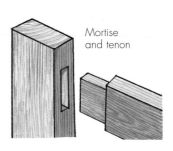

Mortise and tenon

Laps in the T orientation, slot mortised bridle joints, and mortise and tenon joints have a doubled glue surface and an increased resistance to racking.

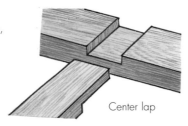

Center lap

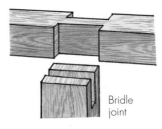

Bridle joint

Mortise and tenon

Choosing and Using Mortise and Tenon

There are hundreds of variations of the mortise and tenon. In each design, whether a frame, leg assembly, or carcass joint, the requirements change, and the joint is modified to meet them. Variations take into consideration the material, the mortise type and mating tenon for structure and style. Other factors include the shoulders suited to joint stability and design and the reinforcements needed against stress.

Tenons are weakest against tension. Without a glue bond, they are simple to pull out of the mortise. Pinning or wedging prevents this and adds mechanical strength to the joint.

Pinning is simple: just a dowel, screw, or peg through the assembled joint and maybe a decorative plug at the surface. But over long years of wood movement, pinning risks splitting the mortised part without a film finish to slow down moisture exchange. Wedging, if the mortise is splayed or the tenon is run through and itself mortised for a wedge or key, creates a mechanical resistance to tension that isn't likely to fail unless the material is destroyed.

Modifications to tenons and shoulders, shown here and in Chapter 2, are the main tactics used to stabilize the joint against twisting and racking.

Sometimes a tenon design will stabilize the project itself.

Certain tenon designs have evolved and have been refined to fill specific needs, such as the haunch used in frame-and-panel construction which fills the panel groove showing in the end of the stile. Mortise and tenon leg and stretcher joints also have histories, ranging from medieval traveling trestle tables, run through and "tusked" or wedged without glue for easy disassembly, to the bridle joint used to join the front legs and apron of a classic demi-lune table.

The internal structures of cabinets, including drawer rails and shelves, use the mortise and tenon, but the design of the joint isn't as well suited to corner carcass joints in solid wood as some others, notably the dovetail.

Stabilizing the Mortise and Tenon

A thick tenon may resist twist but remove too much mortise material; a thin one is proportionately weak and has too much end grain that won't be supported by gluing.

Twin tenons, whose mortises should run lengthwise with the grain, greatly improve against twist, and work even better against rack with an edge shoulder.

The Mortise and Tenon in Frames

A secret sloped haunch is optional on a framing tenon for a rabbeted panel, but one shoulder will be set back the depth of the rabbet.

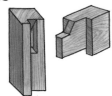

Reinforcing Mortise and Tenon Against Tension

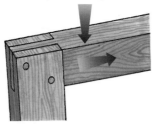

To tighten or splay the tenon so it can't be withdrawn, through tenons are slotted to received wedges, and the mortise is sometimes tapered wider on the side opposite insertion.

Tenon wedge patterns

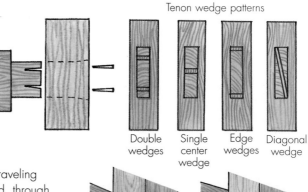

Double wedges | Single center wedge | Edge wedges | Diagonal wedge

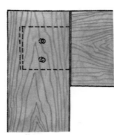

Pins inserted through an assembled bridle joint reinforce against loading and tension, while pins into a draw-bored mortise and tenon pull the joint tight by aligning slightly offset holes.

A joint from traveling furniture of old, through tenons that are themselves mortised to receive single or double tapered wedges reinforce against tension but are removable for disassembly.

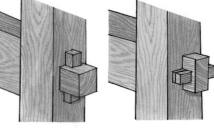

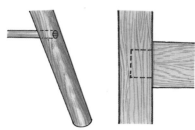

In a frame, the panel groove is filled by a haunch, giving rack resistance like a shoulder plus twist resistance while keeping the tenon back from the end.

Tongued shoulders assist the stability of the joint and the material by restraining movement near the surface.

When a tenoned stretcher lacking shoulder area is run through and wedged, it gains some rack resistance that is built into a wide-shouldered tenon with a large long-grain glue area.

On a wide tenon, a haunch assists against twisting and gives some glue surface but reduces the amount of material removed for the mortise, keeping the part strong.

The Mortise and Tenon in Leg Assemblies

To join chair seat rails to angle in toward the back, the tenon is angled if it can retain some continuous long grain, or the mortise is angled instead.

Stretcher tenons can extend beyond the mortise for decoration or for function, as in a trestle table's wedged through tenon.

In table legs, meeting tenons can be lapped or mitered, but one face shoulder aligns the apron flush with the leg; narrower shoulders may make mortise walls too thin.

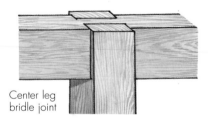

Center leg bridle joint

The bridle joint is commonly used to allow the apron to run through a center table leg (above), or to join the foot of a trestle table (below).

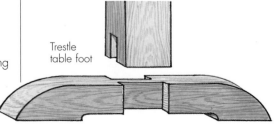

Trestle table foot

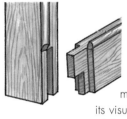

A molded edge frame can be rabbeted or grooved to receive the panel, but the molding is mitered so its visual line continues around the inside of the frame.

A separate loose or slip tenon simplifies shoulder cuts and fitting; mortises are machined with one bit and tenons cut from a strip of material

The short grain weakness of arched rails where they meet the stiles is solved by angling tenon shoulders, or the tenon itself is modified to meet joint requirements.

The Mortise and Tenon in Carcasses

Drawer rails are commonly stub-tenoned into the side of the carcass when the structure doesn't require them to hold in the sides against bowing.

Tenons without face shoulders can be run through and wedged to join shelves to carcass sides.

In a variation of a housed joint, a full or partial housing is mortised and mating tenons are cut in the shelf end or tongue.

71 CHOOSING AND USING MORTISE AND TENON

Blind Mortising

The standard width of a mortise in edge grain is about one third the stock thickness. This proportion varies since the mortise is usually matched to the mortising chisel closest to one third the stock thickness. But too wide a mortise and the cheeks are weak; too narrow and the tenon is weak, so this proportion is a general guide.

Chopping a mortise entirely by hand takes practice for accurate results. Scribing the layout lines deeper once they are placed lets the first chisel cuts remove the waste cleanly, leaving a good guiding shoulder for the chisel. Chiseling tiny bevels in the mortise waste (like those used to guide the saw in Making a Basic Tenon by Hand, pages 76–77) also help to guide a good chop.

Tenon length is just short of blind mortise depth, generally about ¾ the way through the material. A piece of tape on the mortising chisel is enough of a depth gauge. A mortise by hand won't be perfectly flat at the bottom, but it isn't important since it gives the glue somewhere to escape and the tenon end grain isn't a useful bond.

Cut all mortises and then fit tenons to them. It's much easier to shave a little off a tenon cheek than a mortise cheek. Blind tenons too loose can be shimmed with a piece of veneer.

Making a Blind Mortise by Hand

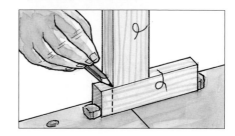

1 With trued faces and edges aligned, outline the tenon part onto the mortise part, leaving a temporary horn to prevent splitting if the mortise should fall at a corner.

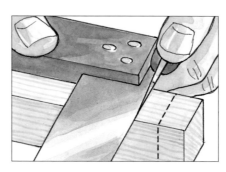

2 Locate the mortise length within the outline of the tenon part, insetting for any shoulders, and scribe each mortise end square across from the trued face with a knife.

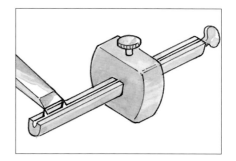

3 Set the spurs of the mortise marking gauge to the chisel width nearest ⅓ the stock thickness; leave at least ¼ of the stock for each mortise cheek.

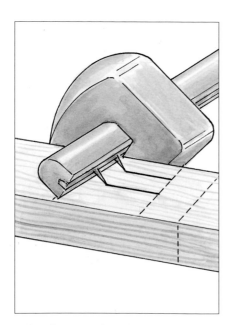

4 Referencing from the marked face, adjust the gauge fence to position the mortise width on the stock thickness and scribe it between the squared end lines.

5 Clamp the part over a bench leg and stand a square nearby to visually aid holding the sides and back of the mortise chisel at 90 degrees to the work.

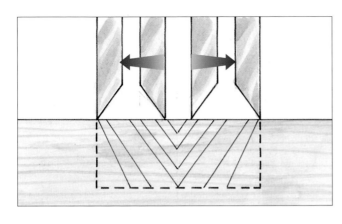

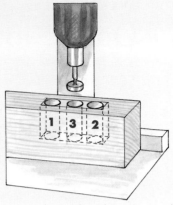

6 One chopping method starts the cuts at the center and they increase in depth as the chisel moves toward the mortise ends and is reversed for the paring end cut.

Use a Forstner bit to clear the waste and reference a flat bottom, plunging the mortise at each end and then the middle, clearing further with the bit and chisels.

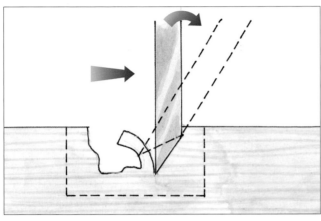

7 In a second method, the chisel chops part way down and leverages the waste on along the mortise and down another layer until last cuts pare waste at the ends.

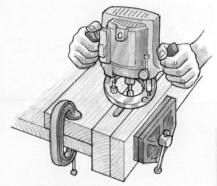

Guide a plunge router along the mortise part while it is clamped in the bench vise and raised flush with another board for clearance and extra router support.

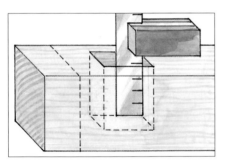

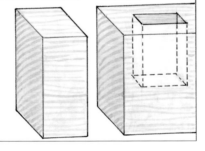

8 Clean up the bottom by leveraging with the chisel and extend a square to check that cheeks are flat and square to the face and the depth is correct.

9 Trim the ends to their mark with a last paring cut to clean up any marred edges from leveraging, glue the joint, then saw off the horn.

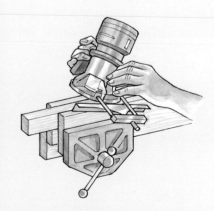

To use a standard router, index the router's fence against high auxiliary vise jaws clamped flush with the mortise part, and carefully tilt the router into the work from the back of its base.

Other Methods for Blind Mortising

The alternative to clearing the waste with a mortising chisel is to drill it out and clean up the cheeks with bench chisels. A brad point bit or Forstner bit works fine, but the Forstner leaves a flat bottom that makes it simple to gauge the mortise depth. Drill press mortising attachments and special square mortising bits eliminate all handwork, as do horizontal boring machines that aren't often found in home workshops.

Routers can be set up to mortise horizontally, but some simpler solutions are shown here. Bits must have a capacity for end cutting, and up-spiral flutes help to clear the chips from the mortise. Several shallow passes are best, determined by the bit size, the material hardness, and the router capacity.

Making Through, Open Slot, or Angled Mortises

The only cautions for through mortising by hand (besides staying square to the face) is against tear-out on the side not covered by tenon shoulders. For this reason, the layout is carried around and worked from each side toward the center.

Making an open slot mortise on the radial arm saw has the advantage of working the part horizontally when it might be too long or heavy for vertical cutting on the tablesaw with a tenoning jig like those shown in this chapter or page 51. The mortise width follows the ⅓ general rule, but it is gauged and marked on the end and down each edge to the tenon width, marked like a shoulder.

When an angled mortise is transferred from a full-size drawing to the part, the mortise width and ends are still scribed into the working edge. The same angled fixture shown for the drill press works for chopping by hand with the chisel kept vertical.

Open Slot Mortise on a Radial-Arm Saw

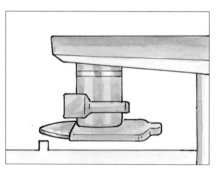

1 Lock a dado head of the desired mortise width in the horizontal position so the outer diameter of the blade aligns exactly with the front of the saw fence.

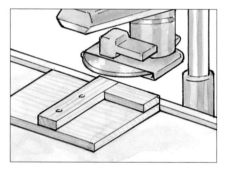

2 Make a sliding jig from scrap plywood and attach a fence square across it plus a scrap to prevent hand slippage into the blade.

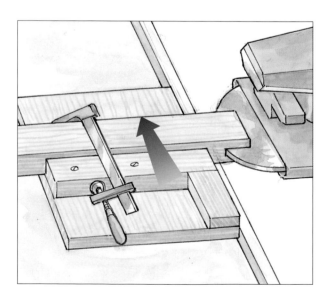

3 Align the blade to waste the mortise by sliding the jig past the blade while feeding the part into it until the marked shoulder lines up with the saw fence's edge.

Through Mortise by Hand

1 Follow the mortise layout steps in Making a Blind Mortise by Hand (see pages 72–73), but this time square the scribed mortise end lines around the part to the opposite face.

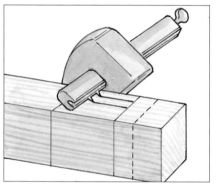

2 Again following those layout steps, mark the mortise width with a gauge, but also mark the width on the opposite face, referencing the fence against the same face while marking.

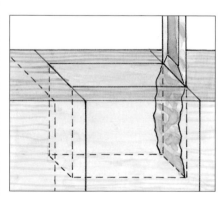

3 Work from each face toward the middle, chopping the waste and forming a slight crown of waste at each end to pare straight and square to the faces to finish.

Angled Mortise on a Drill Press

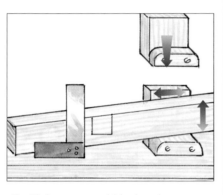

1 From a full-sized drawing of the joint, set a bevel square to the angle of the mortise and use it to mark the angle on the outside of the real part.

2 Slide a stepped block with a rounded shoulder to prevent marring along the length of the part, elevating it until the mortise layout is square to the bench top.

Alternative Methods

To help prevent tear-out when cutting through mortises, first scribe the through mortise layout deep into the shouldered side. This might allow drilling straight through from the opposite side without tear-out. If the part is drilled from both sides, use a fence to position the layout under the bit and keep the same face against the fence for precise alignment.

Handsaw an open slot mortise on the center waste side of the layout. An alternative to drilling a hole to release the waste is to chop it out with a chisel after sawing. Working from each side toward the center, chop down into the waste and split pieces out from the end grain.

An overhand routing box can be used to cut angled mortises. Similar to a hand miter box without saw slots, such a fixture can be modified with a hinged ledge set by a thumbscrew for holding the part to be mortised. Set the angle from a drawing and mark it on the end, adjusting the part until the mortise sides are square to the bench top. Mortises angled longitudinally must be tilted up square, as when drilling out waste on the drill press. To rout a mortise with fixture, the part is clamped to one side of the box while the router rides on top and its fence bears on one side.

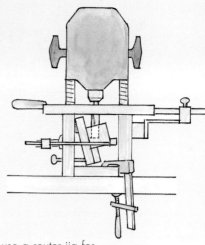

To use a router jig for angled mortises, mark the mortise angle on the part and adjust the jig until the mortise is square to the table, then rout it out.

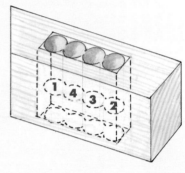

Clear through mortise waste by drilling part way through from each side with a brad point bit, then pare the cheeks flat with chisels.

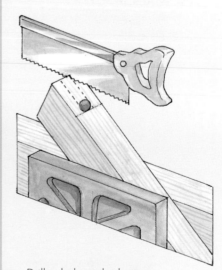

Drill a hole at the bottom of the slot mortise so the waste will release when the slot is sawn following the same procedures as tenon sawing.

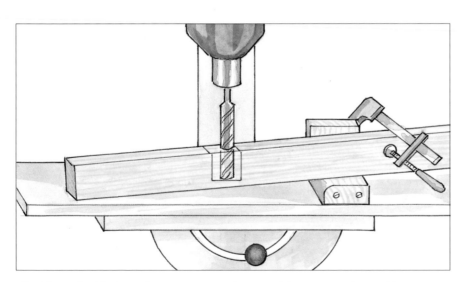

3 Clamp the block in place, supporting the assembly on an auxiliary table if necessary; set the bit depth from the marked layout and waste the mortise, then pare it clean.

Making a Basic Tenon

Opinions differ on the best sequence for sawing tenons. One school of thought holds that first sawing the shoulders risks weakening the tenon by severing long grain if sawing goes too deep. By sawing the cheeks first, the worst consequence of oversawing is a small visible saw kerf on the wood's edge after assembly.

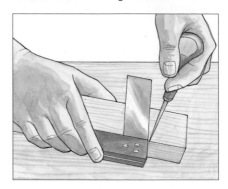

1 From the trued edge, scribe a shoulder square across the part's face, then square the line around, marking all the shoulders and the tenon length to fit the mortise depth.

On the other hand sawing the shoulders first is preferred when a part is tenoned at both ends because the shoulders establish the length of it. There is no repair for a shoulder cut too short as there is for shimming a cheek, so the crucial cut is made first before too much work is invested.

Tenon length should be just under mortise depth. It's easier to gauge a consistent tenon length from its shoulders than a hand-cut mortise depth to leave a little space for glue at the bottom. A tenon swollen with glue acts like a piston in a blind mortise, compressing glue that can split the wood under clamping if it has nowhere to escape or when clamps are tightened too quickly.

Break the leading edges of a tenon with sandpaper or a file to make it easier to insert into the mortise. If the tenon runs through, leave a little extra length so the broken edges don't sink in around the shoulders of the mortise on the through side. Plane or sand the extra length flush after glue-up, unless it is to be left proud for decorative reasons.

Cut multiple parts to length and clamp them together to scribe the shoulders square across all the parts at once. This is especially important for parts that will be in the same frame, on opposite sides of a table, or between opposite pairs of legs. This ensures an accurate structure.

2 Set the mortise marking gauge slightly over the mortise width and adjust the fence to locate and score the tenon thickness around the part from the marked face.

Other Tenoning Methods

The methods for machining basic tenons are similar to those for making end laps, shown in Chapter 4 (see page 52). The only difference is in the layout and cutter adjustment, since two cheeks are usually cut instead of one. The adjustable jig that rides in the miter gauge slot is a variation of the fence straddling jig shown earlier. Runners in grooves between the halves of the jig keep it square.

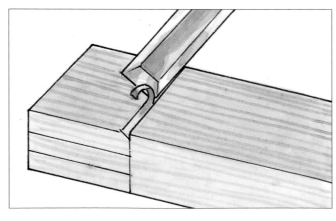

3 Score the shoulder lines deeper and use a chisel to pare a small bevel along the waste of the face shoulders to guide the saw.

4 Hold the part and cleat of a bench hook between thumb and fingers and use the index finger to steady the saw, then saw the shoulder to the tenon line.

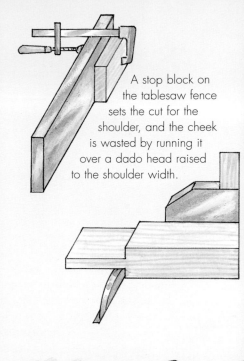

A stop block on the tablesaw fence sets the cut for the shoulder, and the cheek is wasted by running it over a dado head raised to the shoulder width.

5 Clamp the tenon upright and tilted away to saw down the layout lines, steadying the saw with a thumb to keep the kerf in the waste side of the material.

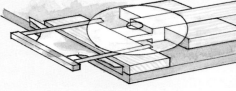

6 The first cuts make a kerf that guides the second cut when the part is reversed in the vise for sawing; a third cut removes the remainder.

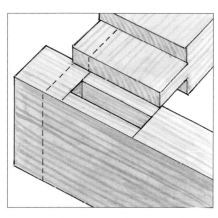

A router can waste tenon cheeks using a jig made of scrap wood attached to plywood to hold the part and support the router, which is stopped at the shoulder by its edge guide.

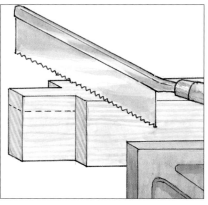

7 Align the tenon to the mortise layout and mark the cutting line for the third shoulder, gauging each successive part from its own mortise.

8 Cut the third shoulder down to the marked line, being careful not to saw into the face shoulders, then saw along the tenon grain and remove the waste.

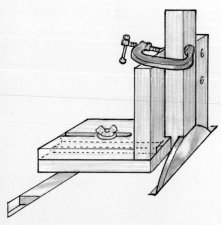

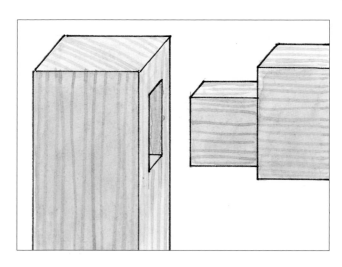

9 Pare the tenon with bench chisels to fit into the mortise with hand pressure, or use a rabbet plane to smooth saw marks and seat the shoulders around the mortise.

After first kerfing shoulders with a tablesaw blade lowered to shoulder width, an adjustable tenoning jig can ride in the miter gauge slot to waste each cheek from the outside.

Reinforcing Tenons Against Tension

When the load on a structure puts the mortise and tenon in tension, the glue bond is the only thing that keeps the joint together unless the joint is reinforced. Pinning, wedging, and wedging with a key or tusk are the basic methods for increasing resistance to tension on the joint.

Splaying the exiting side of a through mortise and kerfing the tenon for one or more wedges is a sure sign of durable hand joinery. Run wedges of a contrasting wood across the grain of the mortise to keep it from splitting. Make the wedge no wider than the tenon thickness. Wedges too wide will bite irreparably into the cheek of the mortise and forever draw attention to the error. For thicker wedges, don't use a saw kerf. Instead, remove small sections of the tenon in a shallow "V" shape. Another method leaves the tenon unkerfed and places the wedges on either side of it at the mortise ends.

Tenons can be draw-bored for a tapered pin so tapping home draws the joint tight. Sometimes the taper is square and pounded in to lock in the material. If draw-boring is used on a slot mortise, align the second hole to pull the tenon in and down in the mortise. Draw-boring is more likely to appear in rustic furniture, green wood projects, or timber framing than refined work.

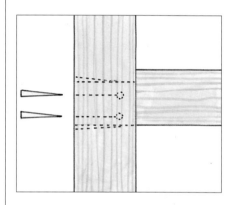

4 Make the jig described in the sidebar to cut wedges with the grain from stock the same thickness as the tenon, flipping the stock for each cut.

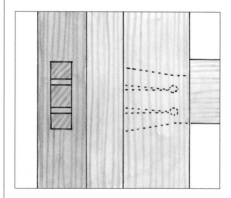

5 Glue the joint and clamp the shoulders home temporarily until the cheeks are clamped, then tap the glued wedges in, alternating taps so they penetrate to equal depth.

Through Wedged Tenon

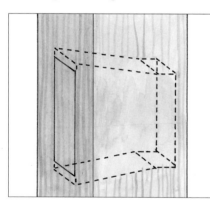

1 Add about 1/16" to each end of the mortise length and taper the end cheeks toward the front, leaving a flat where the tenon enters.

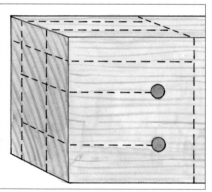

2 Lay out tenon cheeks, shoulders, and wedge locations, then drill a small hole about 1/4 of the tenon length from the shoulder to locate the bottom of each wedge slot.

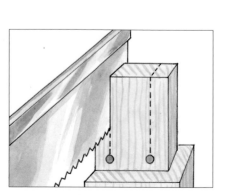

3 First saw the tenon cheeks and shoulders, then saw down the cheek to the small holes that will prevent splitting when the wedges are inserted.

6 When the glue is dry, remove the clamp from the cheeks and saw off any existing wedges, then sand or plane the joint flush.

Draw-Bored Tenon

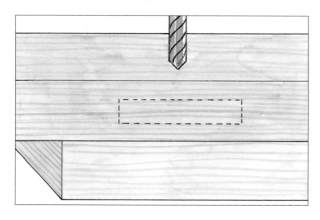

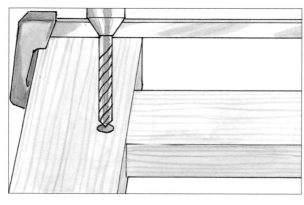

1 Lay out the mortise and back it up with scrap to drill a hole at the center of the mortise length, back about ¼ the stock width from the edge.

2 After cutting the mortise and tenon as usual, assemble and clamp the joint, then insert the drill bit into the hole just to mark its location on the tenon.

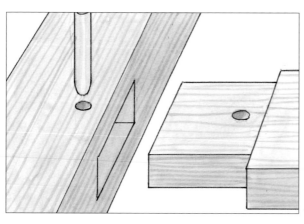

3 Drill a hole in the tenon *slightly* closer to the shoulder than the bit mark, then assemble the joint and drive a tapered peg into it to pull it home.

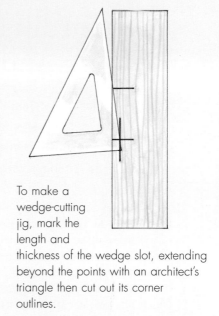

To make a wedge-cutting jig, mark the length and thickness of the wedge slot, extending beyond the points with an architect's triangle then cut out its corner outlines.

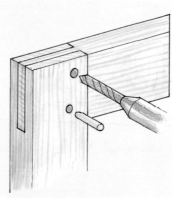

After the joint is glued and dried, pin it by drilling through the mortise part close to the tenon shoulder, inserting some doweling with glue and trimming it flush.

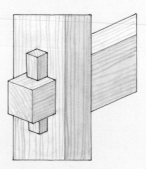

A tusked tenon can be assembled with glue, or without it if the furniture is designed for disassembly. (See Chapter 9, Fasteners, Knockdown Joints, and Hardware.)

More About Reinforcements

To cut wedges on a tablesaw, use a simple piece of plywood scrap with the wedge taper cut into the edge like a notch. With the workpiece in the notch, the plywood can run along the fence as the blade cuts the wedge. Such a jig can also position work for a handsaw. Wedges are always cut with the grain, otherwise tapping in will snap them. The architect's triangle simplifies layout and doubles as a tool for setting the angle of sawblades.

Pins through the joint should be placed near the shoulder because they restrict wood movement and eventually may split in the mortise part if the species isn't very stable. Keep the diameter of the reinforcing pins small, but larger flush round plugs or round or square pegheads left proud can be used for a decorative accent.

Angled Tenons and Shoulders

Angled tenons or shoulders are common where stretchers join tapered or canted table legs and where chair seat rails and stretchers join chair legs. Full-sized drawings are indispensable aids for setting up layout tools and determining measurements when joinery angles vary from 90 degrees.

The edge or face shoulders of an angled tenon aren't square to the stock, but the tenon is usually laid out square to the angled shoulder so the mortise can be made square to its stock. Its angled shoulder turns the tenon oblique to the grain. An angled tenon must contain some continuous long grain for strength. Drawings help to visualize this and work out the size of tenon within the stock dimensions.

An angled-shoulder tenon is longer on one edge than the other, or longer on one cheek than the other. The tenon stays in line with the grain, and the mortise has to be angled to mate with the shoulder. Depending how the angled mortise is made, the end of the tenon stays square across its width or it may be angled. A sliding T-bevel is a fundamental tool for angled layouts, and it also can transfer angled settings to machines.

Angled Tenon

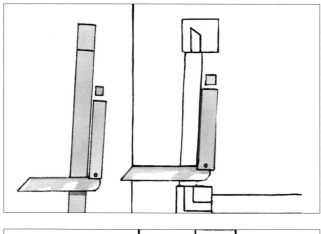

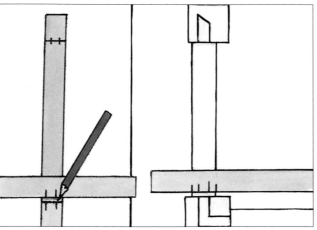

1 Transfer the edge shoulder angle with a bevel square from the full-sized drawing to overlong stock, marking the shoulders the correct distance apart.

2 Measure or use a story stick to transfer the mortise offset and tenon thickness from the drawing to the part on the angled shoulder marks.

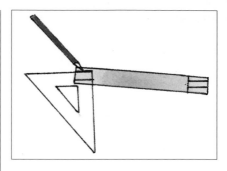

3 Align the square corner of an architect's triangle to the shoulder mark and extend the marks for the tenon thickness along the part's edge.

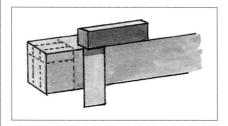

4 Square the face shoulders across and connect the edge shoulder angle on the opposite edge, extend tenon outlines from that angle, mark tenon thickness on the end, then saw it.

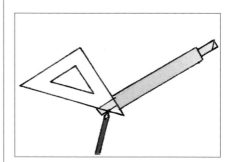

5 For mitered tenons, after the tenon and third shoulder are cut, mark tenon length and use an architect's triangle to scribe the miter cut on the tenon end.

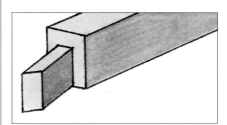

6 Trim off the tenon end at a 45-degree angle and clean up the cheeks and shoulders as done for any other tenon.

Angled Shoulder

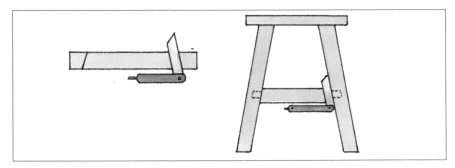

1 Cut the stock to length and transfer the shoulder angle and location from the full-sized drawing to it, then use the angle to set the miter gauge on the tablesaw.

2 Raise a dado head to shoulder width and waste cheek 1, flip the stock for cheek 2, then reset the miter gauge on the right to cut 3 and 4.

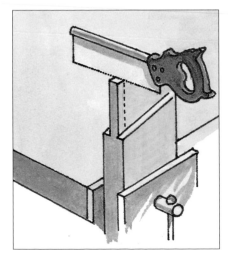

3 Saw down the tenon to trim it to width and across the edge shoulders, following the angle, to release the waste.

More Angled Tenons

Handsaw or bandsaw angled tenons like any other. On the radial arm saw, turn the blade horizontal and use a height table under the part. The tilt direction of tablesaws vary, and so might the height of tenon shoulders from the table. Choose what works best, either tilting the blade and using a vertical tenoning jig, or keeping the blade vertical and tilting the part as shown in the sidebar.

To cut angled tenons with a router, use an angled router step jig with two tiers and cleats underneath to align the part for wasting the tenon cheeks to the shoulder. The second tier is set back the distance from the outer diameter of the bit to the edge of the router sub-base. Do this by careful measuring or more simply by attaching the second tier slightly farther back and then have it guide the router to trim the edge of the first tier exactly in line with the bit.

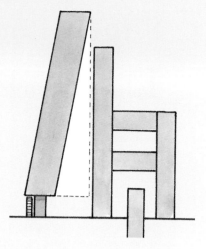

Taking the taper angle from full-size plans, set the tenon cheek angle with a wood wedge on a vertical fence sliding jig.

After kerfing the shoulders, align the tenon cheek layout to the blade with an adjustable tilting hinged jig that runs in the miter gauge slot.

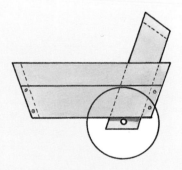

To cut cheeks with a router, use a stepped jig cut to the shoulder angle; the router is guided and stopped by the step on the jig.

Slip or Loose Tenons

I t's easy to confuse the name "slip tenon" with an open slot mortise or slip joint and the name "loose tenon" with a through tenon that is reinforced with a key or tusk but not glued. The same terms refer to different joints. Here a slip or loose tenon is a joint composed of two mortised parts bridged by a separate, floating tenon.

Loose tenons are based on machine joinery techniques. A round bit whose diameter equals the mortise width is plunged in at one end of the mortise, moved along the mortise length to cut it, and pulled out, leaving rounded mortise ends. Confusingly, this type of mortise is called a slot mortise, but is not the same as the open slot mortise.

In the home shop, these mortises are usually cut by a router or drill press, then strips of tenon stock are sized to fit the mortise. The stock's square edge or the mortise's round end are modified to match, and the tenons are cut to length and glued. A loose tenon is also the repair for a damaged tenon, which can be cut off, mortised out, and a new tenon made to fit.

Making a Slip or Loose Tenon

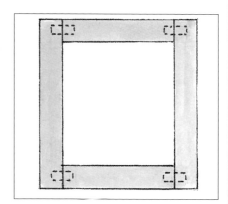

1 Make a full-size drawing to determine the part widths and lengths and mortise and tenon placement, then cut the stiles to length and the rails to the length between them.

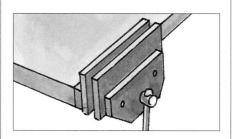

2 Clamp one corner's rail vertically in the vise and line up its stile horizontally to mark mortises simultaneously on the rail end and stile edge, and repeat for each corner.

3 Set up for one of the methods shown in Blind Mortising on page 72, in this case auxiliary vise jaws attached through the bolt holes and extending the jaw height.

4 Clamp the workpiece flush with the vise jaws, align an end-cutting straight bit with the router edge guide set against the jaw, and cut each mortise in several passes.

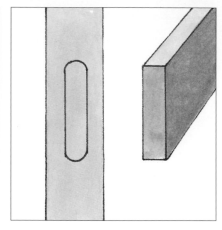

5 Mill a length of tenon stock that is as wide as the length of the mortise and as thick as the width of it.

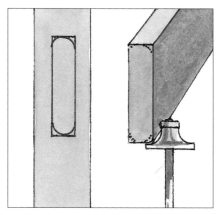

6 Match the tenon stock to the mortise either by squaring the mortise corners or by rounding the edges of the tenon stock.

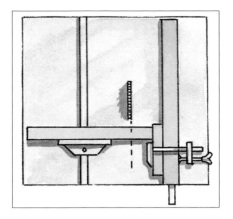

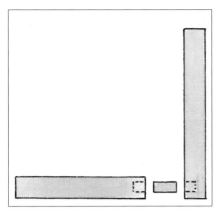

7 Set up a stop block on the saw fence to repeat cut tenons that are slightly less than double the depth of the mortise.

8 Spread glue in the mortises and on the tenon and assemble each joint, then clamp the frame.

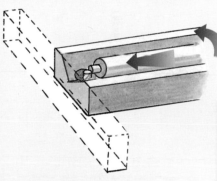

Using a corner jig that lowers with the drill press table is one way to end-cut with a plug cutter to make a round tenon after shoulders are kerfed.

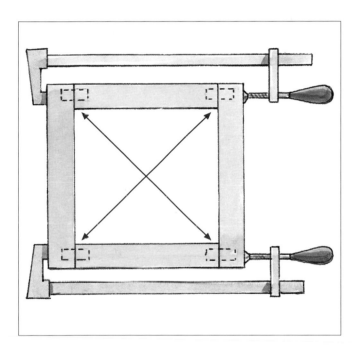

9 Adjust the clamps until each diagonal measures the same, ensuring that the frame is square, and let dry undisturbed.

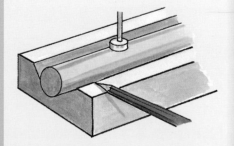

An over-sized hole in a V-block lets a router table straight bit through to cut the tenon and also allows adjustment from the fence stop to control tenon length.

Round Tenons and Round Stock

Round tenons are also made loose by drilling into both parts and using dowel pins or doweling rod as tenons, the machine-based dowel joint covered in Chapter 8 (see page 123). To make an integral round tenon, center a plug cutter on the part's end on the drill press or lathe after kerfing in the shoulders.

One method is shown for routing a round end tenon horizontally, but vertical routing is possible with ball-bearing rabbeting bits and a jig. The

work is done either end up with the part held stationary and the router handheld and moving, or end down with the part held by a moveable jig and the bit stationary in a router table. Drilling for a round tenon is fairly straightforward, but by using a V-block for marking and holding, a round part can be mortised conventionally and a flat chiseled to accept a rectangular shoulder.

Clamp round stock in a V-block to drill round mortises, or slide a marking device along the edge to make parallel lines for a conventional mortise.

Stabilizing Tenons

Edge and face shoulders on a tenon increase its mechanical resistance to racking. But each shoulder reduces the material in the tenon and replaces it with the shoulder's end grain, which lacks gluing strength. Deep edge shoulders subtract gluing area from the tenon's cheek and make a wide part vulnerable to twisting, which easily breaks the shoulder's end grain bond. Wood movement and shrinking in the joint also stress the glue bond. Haunches and multiple tenons help to overcome these difficulties.

The square profile of a haunch neatly fills the panel groove that runs through the stile's end in frame-and-panel construction. More importantly, the second shallow mortise that houses the haunch lets the edge shoulder into the wood without weakening the end of the part when the tenon falls there. This creates cheeks for long-grain gluing, one of the main purposes of any woodworking joint. The edge shoulders and tenon are then supported mechanically against twisting and properly bonded to the mortise cheeks.

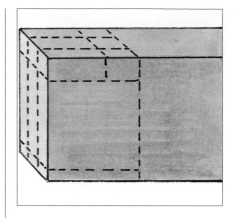

4 Lay out the tenon to fit the mortise and scribe the haunch line across the outside edge forward of the face shoulders an amount equal to the tenon's thickness.

5 Don't saw an edge shoulder on the haunched edge, just saw down the haunch line to the tenon, then saw the face and bottom edge shoulders, and the tenon cheeks.

Haunched Tenon

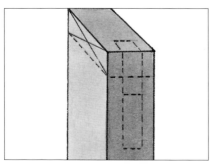

1 Gauge the mortise width on the edge and horn end, marking a depth there equal to the mortise width, and start the mortise its width away from the horn cut-off line.

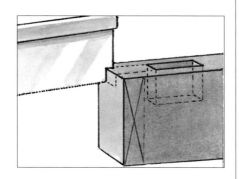

2 After chopping the mortise, saw along the lines extending from it on the horn edge and down the horn end to the depth marked.

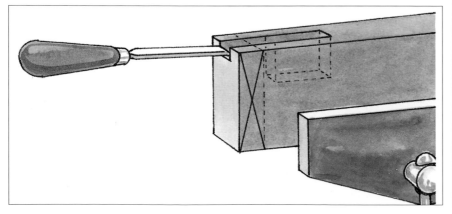

3 Tap a chisel lightly into the end grain between the sawn lines to chip out the waste down to the depth mark, paring the bottom parallel to the face.

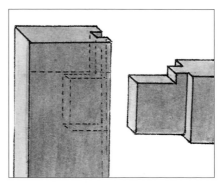

6 Test fit the tenon, making sure neither the haunch nor the tenon length prevent the shoulders from seating, then glue the joint and cut off the horn.

More Stabilizing Tenons

Haunching and dividing wide tenons is another way to preserve the stance of the tenon against twisting without mortising out a lot of material. Mortises for the tenons are overlaid by a second shallow mortise for the haunch. The tenon is made normally and secondary edge shoulders (the haunch) squared across it and cut to fit the shallow mortise. It may be easiest to divide the tenon by cope sawing to the same depth as the haunch.

Twin tenons usually appear on stock more square than rectangular in cross-section. They keep the tenon base wide against twisting, double the glue surface, and proportion the tenons and shoulders to the stock. Orient twin tenons so the load is on the tenon edge, not the face.

In addition to increasing the glue area and widening the tenon stance, theory says a tongued shoulder restrains wood movement close to the joint line. In the old days, tongued shoulders were used in joints under veneer to try to keep movement from buckling the veneer. Now it's just cautious construction.

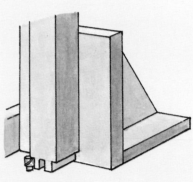

Cut a haunch in a wide tenon and reduce the tenon width to keep the mortise part strong and prevent excessive dimensional conflict from breaking the tenon's glue bond.

Sloped Haunch Tenon

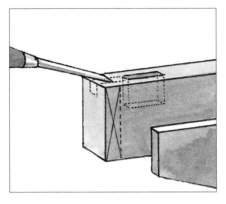

1 Lay out and chop the mortise as for a haunched tenon, then chisel from inside the horn cut-off line, angling down toward the mortise, to reach a depth equal to mortise width.

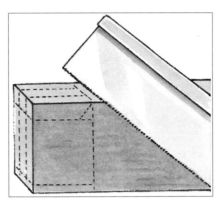

2 Lay out the tenon and make the first saw cut across the top edge, angling from the face shoulder line to a measurement from it equal to the tenon thickness.

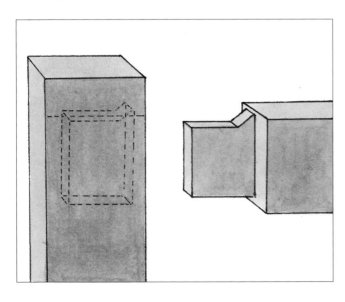

3 Pare the slope slightly down from the top edge (matching its socket started inside the layout), so removing material to flush up the parts after gluing won't expose the slope.

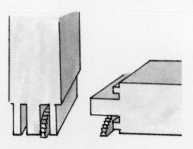

Set up a router table and push block that runs along the fence to waste each shoulder and between the tenons, doubling the gluing surface and increasing the resistance to twisting.

For a tenon that restrains movement at the joint line, cut four saw kerfs for tenon cheeks and shoulders, and thin tongues that are shortened, fit to matching slots and glued.

Special Framing Tenons

The basic joint between a frame and panel is a groove housing or a rabbet housing with a stop holding in the panel. The important thing to know is how frame mortise and tenon accommodate them.

A groove runs centered on the inside edges of the frame, right over the mortises. The groove width is about one third the stock thickness, with its depth about the same as its width to keep the material strong.

The mortise width and tenon thickness match the groove width. Decide this width first and lay out the mortise and tenon cheeks to it. Then mark the groove depth on the end of the tenon stock, allotting the remainder to the tenon and haunch. This determines the length and placement of the mortise on its stock. Mark the frame rabbet on the end of the tenon stock to find the tenon width and so the mortise length and placement. The rabbet should remove about two thirds of the material

thickness to house the panel and stop, and cut into the width of the stock about one third the thickness or more. The tenon shoulder on the face side of the frame is set back to house the lip formed by rabbeting.

Some frames have a molded detail on the inside edge that is continued around, or returned, by mitering. After mortising, run a rabbet to a depth equal to the molding width. But instead of cutting the tenon's face shoulder back to house the lip left on the mortise part, the molded detail is removed flush with the mortise and rabbet, then mitered to match the tenon.

Mortise and Tenon for a Rabbeted Frame

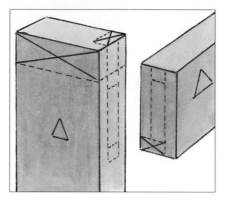

1 Determine the dimensions of the rabbet that will be under the sloped haunch tenon to find the mortise size and placement, then lay out and chop the mortise.

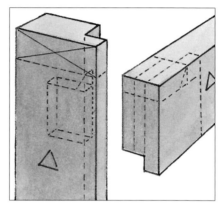

2 Run the rabbet to the face side cheeks of the mortise and tenon and mark the tenon shoulders, setting the face shoulder back to house the lip left by rabbeting.

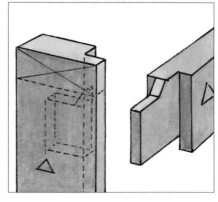

3 Saw the slope of the haunch first, then the two shoulders, the cheeks, and the cuts along the tenon thickness, sawing the horn after the glue dries.

Mortise and Tenon with a Panel Groove

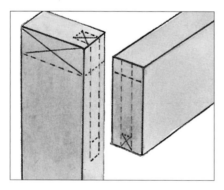

1 Choose a panel groove width, lay out the mortise and tenon cheeks to it, mark its depth under the tenon to find the tenon width, and place the mortise.

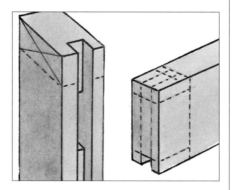

2 Chop the mortise and run the panel groove over it on the inside edges of all parts, then lay out the tenon so the haunch length fills the groove.

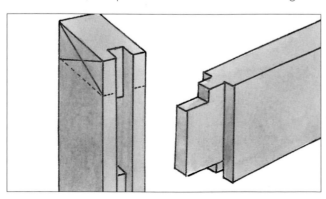

3 Saw the haunch shoulder first, then the face shoulders and tenon cheeks, glue the joint, and saw off the horn.

Mortise and Tenon for a Molded Frame

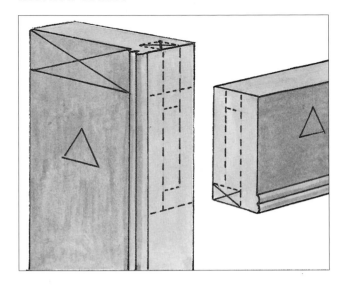

1 Run the molding detail on the inside face edge of the stock, then lay out the rabbet and haunched tenon mortise so they stop in line with the molding detail.

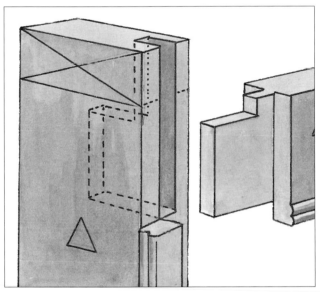

2 Chop the mortise, run the rabbet to the line of the molding detail, finish the tenon layout and saw it, then saw the molding detail away flush with the mortise.

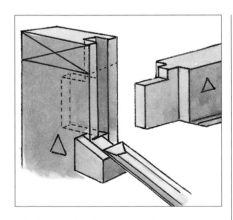

3 Use a 45-degree chisel guide on the edge of the stock to miter the molding detail away from the tenon shoulder and mortise, and then fit the joint together.

More Framing Tenons

Frames for divided panels have tenoned center rails or muntins whose molded detail will run on both edges. Whether the frame is grooved or rabbeted, to return a molding around each separate panel the width of the molding is cut away at the mortise and mitered to match the tenon. Increase the length between tenon shoulders by the width of moldings cut away. Also increase the length by the amount that mitered tenon shoulders are let into mortise parts to prevent weak short grain on arched rails.

A molded detail on a frame for several panels is run on both edges of the center rail or muntin like the groove, and the detail is returned by mitering.

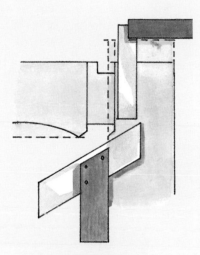

To prevent weak short grain on an arched rail, a small miter is cut on the shoulder of the tenon and housed in the shoulder of the mortise.

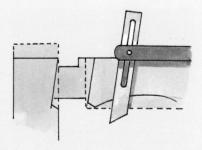

Another method for avoiding weak short grain houses a small miter and an angled tenon shoulder within the profile of the mortise part.

CHAPTER SIX

MITERS
AND BEVELS

Miters and bevels are cuts made
at angles other than 90
degrees. Aesthetically, miters
or bevels can unify a shape visually by
continuing the line of grain around it.
Structurally, miters add softening facets and
bridge the gap between squares and circles.

The term "miter" and "bevel" sometimes
interchange. An important distinction is that
a bevel cut is not perpendicular to the face
of the wood, whereas a miter is either an
exact 45-degree cut (even if it's a bevel) or a
general term for an angled cut.

About Miters and Bevels

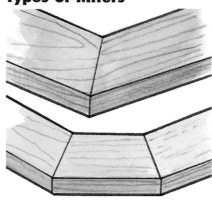

There are three basic types of miters, and they create a fourth type when used in combination. Frame miters angle the blade path across the wood width but the blade tilt is perpendicular to the face. Cross and length miters angle the blade tilt to the face and are really just bevel cuts. The cross miter path is perpendicular to the wood edge, and the length miter path parallel to it. The fourth type is a compound miter. It combines a bevel tilt with an angled path either across or along the grain.

A mitered corner continues the wood grain visually to harmonize with the design.

The glue surface of a length miter is all long grain, but other miters are weak because the glue surface is end grain. Consequently, miters need to be reinforced. And even though the gluing orientation is strong, clamp pressure causes miters to slip out of gluing position unless splines or other mechanical restraints are combined with special clamping techniques.

Inaccurate miter joints are hard to get away with and difficult to correct. Time is well spent on adjusting machines and making tests in scraps before committing to the actual cut.

The angle gauges on stationary machines are often imprecise, so miter joints have spawned an aftermarket business in precision gauges and jigs plus an endless array of shopmade devices and set-up methods that aid accurate work.

Cutting miters and bevels by machine generates extra force that pulls or pushes the wood, encouraging it to slip out of position during cutting. Sharp blades, hold-downs, stops on the miter gauge, and sandpaper on its face all reduce slipping and unnecessary accidents.

Types of Miters

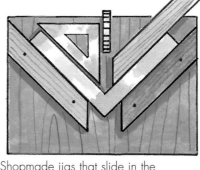

The angle of a frame miter will vary with the number of sides, but the cut is always across the width of the board face.

Setting Up and Checking Miters

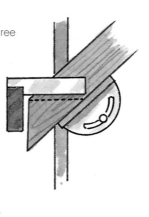

Test a 45-degree miter gauge setting by trimming a scrap end, flipping it for a second cut and then checking the apex of the triangular cut-off for square.

Align the same increment on each framing square leg to the miter gauge slot to set the gauge to 45 degrees, using longer lengths for a more accurate setting.

Gap is twice the error

To check a 45-degree miter square for accuracy, align an architect's triangle to it, then hold the triangle and flip the square so any gap shows double its error.

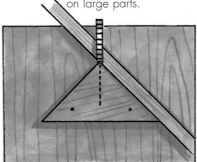

Shopmade jigs that slide in the tablesaw's miter gauge slots or sit fixed on the radial-arm saw table help to cut accurate miters, especially on large parts.

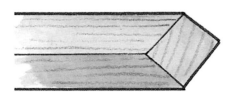

Cross miters are really bevels on the end of the board so it's not unusual to also hear them called end bevels.

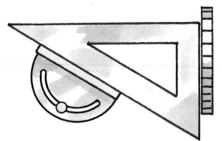

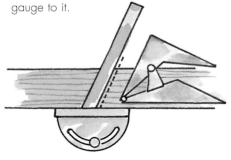

The bevel angle of a length miter (also called an edge bevel) will vary, as all miters do, with the number of sides in the structure.

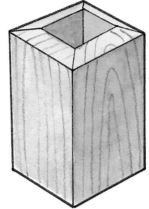

Compound miters combine a bevel cut with a frame miter or a taper cut to make shadow boxes or other slope-sided shapes.

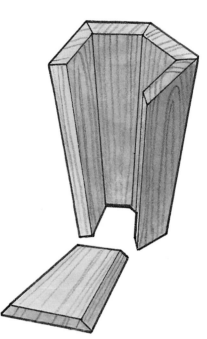

Set angles other than 45 degrees directly from architect's triangles or transfer the angle from a drawing to the wood's underside and set the miter gauge to it.

When angles exceed the miter gauge capacity, an auxiliary fence or tapered block will extend the range of the gauge.

Use a sliding bevel to transfer the bevel angle from a protractor and set the blade tilt or mitering angle on a tablesaw or radial-arm saw.

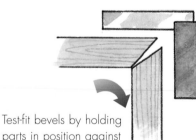

Test-fit bevels by holding parts in position against a square (or a sliding bevel set to a drawing for larger angles), then adjust the blade to correct the bevel.

Figuring Miters and Bevels

No other joinery employs as much mathematics as miters and bevels. Even a simple 45-degree corner miter brings geometric principles to woodwork. Both geometry and trigonometry can be applied to calculate machine settings for precise fits.

The cutting angle for frame miters and bevel joints is calculated by dividing the number of sides into a circle's 360 degrees to find the miter angle. The cutting angle is half that. Depending on the angle or the machine's calibrations, the gauge, blade, or radial arm is set either directly to the cutting angle or to its complement (the remainder when the cutting angle is subtracted from 90 degrees).

To improve on the miter gauge's accuracy, lay out permanent settings for common angles on the tablesaw top using a framing square and a little geometry, first making sure the table-saw blade sits parallel to the miter gauge slots. This can be checked by measuring from the miter gauge slot to the same tooth positioned at the front and rotated to the back of the blade. Once the gauge is checked or adjusted according to the manual, use the method shown to bisect a 90-degree angle for a 45 and further bisect for other common angles.

Extend the miter fence with a straightedge to a point marked on the bisecting line, lock the setting and test the cut for accuracy with layout tools or against a careful drawing. The farther out the testing point is placed along the bisecting line, the finer the adjustments to tune the gauge setting. Punch a permanent small dent in the tabletop when the right setting is found.

Trigonometry (or a lot of trial and error) is useful for accuracy with less common angles. Use it directly to set the miter gauge with a framing square, or to lay out an angle's rise and run on a jig or on paper to transfer to machines with layout tools. Trigonometry will also find the inside or outside length for the frame of an existing object or to fit the frame inside a defined space.

Compound miters require a combination of two settings on the radial-arm or tablesaw. Shown in this chapter are two drafting methods to find the bevel angle and the miter or taper angle.

Miters and Math

The formula for finding miter or bevel cutting angles is: 360 degrees divided by the number of segments divided by two equals the cutting angle.

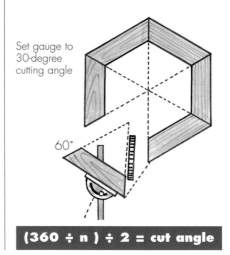

Set gauge to 30-degree cutting angle

60°

(360 ÷ n) ÷ 2 = cut angle

Applying Geometry to Machine Set-Ups

To find a 45-degree angle on the tablesaw, erect a perpendicular to the miter slot and bisect the angle, then punch a dent on the line to use to set the miter fence with a straightedge.

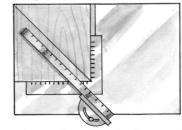

67.5°

22.5°

Bisecting the 45-degree angle above yields an accurate 22.5 degrees; transfer any of the marked angles or complementary angles to a sliding bevel to set blade tilt.

Applying Trigonometry to Mitering

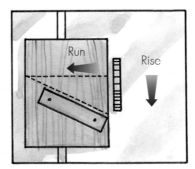

Run

Rise

Trigonometry tables can be used to find the tangent of a desired angle and the ratio of rise to run; the points can then be marked on a sliding jig whose fence is along their hypotenuse.

Trigonometry ratios can also be used to set the miter gauge if the increments of the rise and run on framing square legs are aligned to the miter gauge slot.

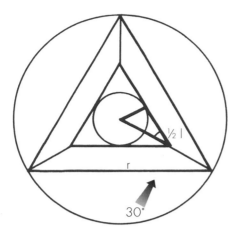

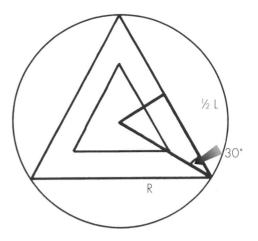

The formula to find the inside length of a concentric, equilateral shape is: Length equals twice the radius divided by the tangent of the miter angle.

$$l = 2r \div \tan \phi$$

The formula to find the outside length of a concentric equilateral shape is: Length equals twice the radius times the cosine of the miter angle.

$$L = 2R \cos \phi$$

Finding Angles by Drafting

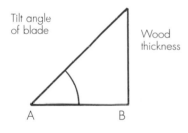

Tilt angle of blade

Wood thickness

A

B

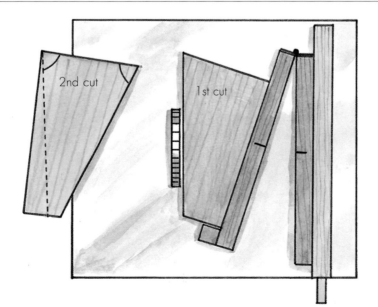

Edge bevel angle

A
B

Miter gauge or radial-arm angle

Lay a compound miter flat to see the true shape and the miter angle, then erect perpendicular AB, measure, and scale with the wood thickness to find the blade tilt.

2nd cut

1st cut

Open a taper jig's legs to the slope per foot 12" from the pivot point, rip the taper angle, then double the opening and flip the board to make the second cut.

Frame Miters

Miters cut across the grain with the blade perpendicular to the wood's face allow framing of panels, fields, or pictures in a flat plane. The common 45-degree miter makes a rectilinear shape with four sides. Six- or eight-sided shapes are also familiar and form the basis for further shaping into oval and round frames like those used as tabletop banding.

A simple frame miter is an end grain butt joint whose only strength comes from the type of glue holding it together. A very light frame glued with epoxy might survive a low-stress application, but most frame miters need reinforcement to last.

Frame miter reinforcements are either an integral part of the joint or enhance an assembly after glue-up. Splines or joinery that creates long-grain glue surfaces like the lap miter are the common integral reinforcements, and others are shown in Chapter 8 (see pages 122, 126).

Dadoes for splines are run in the mitered ends prior to glue-up by whatever method is most convenient given the length of the parts. Short parts can run supported on end over the tablesaw blade or over a straight bit on a router table. Longer parts are more convenient to work face down with a router spline cutter or on a radial-arm saw.

Alternatively, after a butt-glued assembly dries, the mitered frame can be carefully reinforced by nails, feathers, gussets, or butterfly keys (shown in Chapter 7, page 114). When frames are built around a plywood panel or field like a tabletop which has no risk of seasonal movement, gluing the frame parts to the panel groove or rabbet will reinforce the glued miters.

Similar to the radial-arm technique shown here, a decorative hand technique for feathering frame corners is to handsaw two or three kerfs and glue contrasting veneer into them. If nails are used, drive them into the miter through the frame sides so the weight of the frame doesn't pull them out.

Professional framers saw miters close to length and use expensive guillotine devices to pare the joint smooth. In the home shop, skilled use of handplanes and miter shooting boards are the best alternative.

Frame Miter by Hand

1 Mark 45 degrees with a layout tool or scribe the diagonal of a square whose sides equal the wood width and clamp a block there to guide the saw.

Feathered Miter on a Radial-Arm Saw

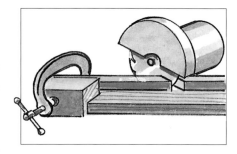

1 Set the arm to the miter angle and cut one end of each part, then clamp a stop block on the fence to exactly gauge the final cut to length.

Lap Miter

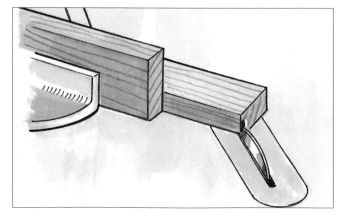

1 Cut the parts to final length and set the depth of cut to half the thickness, then kerf across the face corner of the frame stiles (the vertical parts) at 45 degrees.

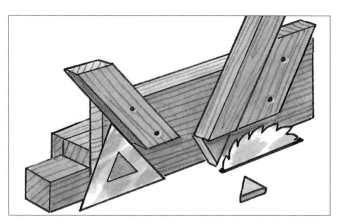

2 Use a sliding fence jig with stops at 45 degrees to the saw table to cut away half the thickness of the kerfed corners without touching the shoulders.

2 Lightly shave the joint of saw marks on a miter shooting board with a rabbet or other plane, shimming a playing card between the fence and part to correct misfits.

3 Heavily coat the end grain with glue then clamp the frame using a method like this adjustable shopmade device that keeps the parts from sliding out of position when clamp force is applied.

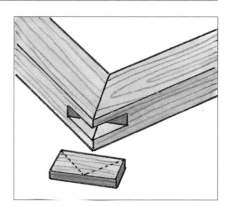

2 Turn the saw horizontal, extending the blade about ⅓ into the miter's length, and kerf through the frame's glued corners by sliding them into the blade on a height table.

3 Thickness a strip of key material to fit the kerf and cut lengths and glue them in, then trim with a saw and sand flush after drying.

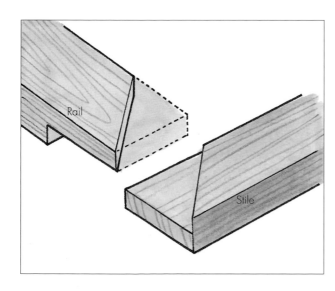

3 Cut square end laps (see Chapter 4, page 52) on the horizontal rails and trim the halved portion to 45 degrees to fit against the shoulder of each stile end.

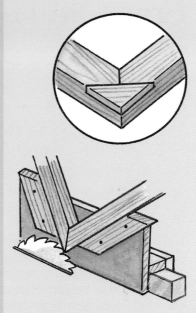

Feather a miter on the tablesaw with the help of a fence jig or just remove a portion of the corner's back side and glue in a reinforcing gusset.

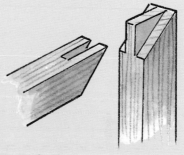

A bridle miter doubles the glue surface of a lap miter when the stile is shouldered on both sides and the rail is slot mortised and mitered to fit.

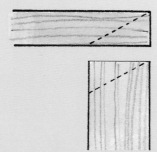

Mitering will accommodate frame members of different widths if the miter angle is drawn on one part and transferred to the other with a sliding bevel.

Cross Miters

Cross miters made by bevel cuts across the grain are, like frame miters, inherently weak joints because of their end grain glue surface. Fortunately, also like frame miters, they are used more in supplemental rather than structural capacities. Most of the reinforcing techniques that are used on frame miters also apply to cross miters, but the decorative butterfly key is eliminated and replaced by the dovetail key, which makes mock dovetails of the cross miter.

With end grain to end grain in an L orientation, a cross miter is hard to modify for long-grain contact except by combining it with the finger joint shown in Chapter 4 (see page 58). Even internal splines don't make long-grain contact unless the joint is part of a 6- or 8-sided structure where the joint angle is greater than 120 degrees. Feathering through the corners does bring long-grain strength to cross miters.

The tablesawn lock-miter joint shown here automatically interlocks the joint so it depends less on glue strength, but it's only effective when it's correctly oriented to resist tension. Lock miters are a common joint for drawers because they're strong against pulling on the drawer front and show no end grain on the front or side.

The house rabbet miter adds no long-grain glue surface to a cross miter joint. Its slight shoulder adds a little glue shearing strength and some assistance against racking, but real strength comes from pins driven through the joint from the outside or from making the joint long-grain. The pinned housed rabbet miter is a common drawer joint in Japan; it is simple, strong, and decorative if contrasting pins are used. The advantage of the housed rabbet miter is that it can join different thicknesses of wood.

The width of splines in cross and other miters should be about twice the wood thickness and kept inside the centerline of the joint. To cut dadoes for the splines, hold the wood face flat on the tablesaw and use the same tilt angle that cut the bevel. If an angled fence tilts the bevel flat against the table, the cutter is upright at 90 degrees. Stopped splines are easiest made by router.

Housed Rabbet Miter

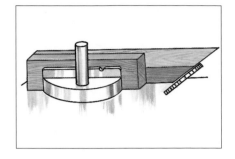

1 Using material that is the same thickness as its mating corner (or thinner like this drawer side) bevel the end to 45 degrees.

Locked Miter

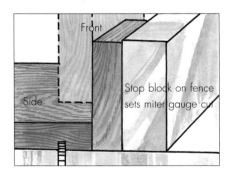

1 Set the blade in line with the thickness of the front and kerf on the inside face of the side with the blade height about ⅓ of the side's thickness.

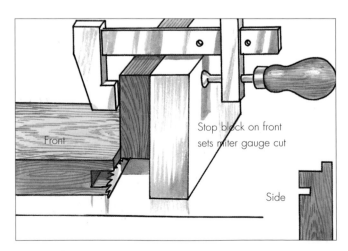

4 Use a normal blade lowered to cut only the narrow tongue in the front, trimming it to the depth of the dado kerfed ⅓ into the side thickness.

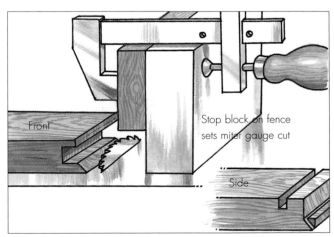

5 Tilt the blade to 45 degrees and use a stop block on the fence to control the beveling of projecting tongues on the front and side.

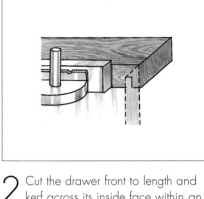

2 Cut the drawer front to length and kerf across its inside face within an outline of the side's thickness and just to the height of its bevel.

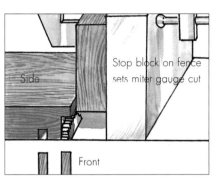

3 Tilt the blade to 45 degrees to remove the waste inside the front and glue the joint together, reinforcing when dry with pins through the side.

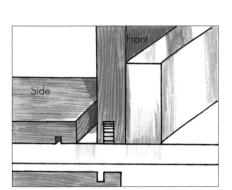

2 Dado to the height of the side thickness at a width about half the front thickness, leaving a narrow tongue to fit the side's kerf.

3 Set a stop block on the fence, lower the dado blade to ⅔ the thickness, then cut a rabbet that leaves a tongue to fit the dado in the front.

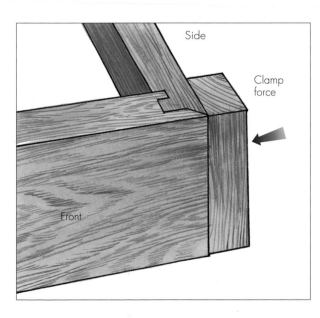

6 Unlike most miters, a lock miter needs clamp force to be applied in only one direction, but a block should distribute the pressure on the miter itself.

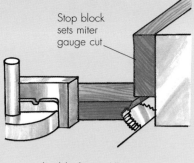

Leave the blade at 45 degrees to kerf for splines in the outer ¾ of the end grain glue surface of 45 degree cross miters.

Cross miters at other than 45 degrees are splined on end on the router table or tablesaw with the blade square and the bevel riding flat on the table.

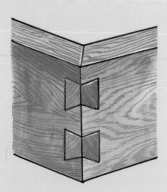

Mock dovetails are a decorative way to reinforce cross miters as explained in Chapter 7 (see page 114).

Length Miters

A plain bevel joint along the grain brings a certain air of harmony to joinery, probably because the joint line blends so well with the material that the parts merge into a single unit. Length miters (or bevel joints) also bring with them the new world of segmented joinery populated by umbrella stands, planters, and kaleidoscopes. Length miters have a grain orientation that is strong for gluing once the parts are persuaded to cooperate with clamping.

Length miters have a long glue line and the bevel angle will slip under pressure. Splines (page 40) or biscuits (page 126) stop the slipping but it is still difficult to keep the joint from opening up on the inside or outside if clamp force is misdirected. Especially when the construction has more than the four segments found in box shapes, gluing up bevel joints is easier to do in stages, two parts at a time.

Pinch dogs will hold the parts in position while more pressure is applied, but the dogs will leave holes in the wood. Band clamps, rope tied in a circle and tightened by twisting a stick, or even strips of old bicycle tire tubes that are wrapped around like giant rubber bands can be used to join pairs of mitered parts. Place blocks to put the pressure where it's needed.

A self-squaring joint like the rabbet miter with its inside step to butt the miters and keep the joint in position is a helpful choice for square structures. Still, the outside corner of the miter benefits from corner clamping blocks to press it tight. This joint is possible on a router table with a straight bit and a chamfering bit, but to be made on the radial-arm saw, it requires the dangerous ripping position.

The waterfall joint capitalizes on a miter's ability to carry the grain around a turn. It's particularly good in custom veneered plywood cabinets where the back is seen. The back is taken from the center of the sheet, the ends joined to it by a waterfall, and the face frame attached.

Waterfall Joint

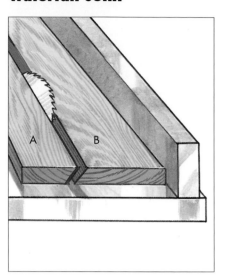

1 Tilt the blade to 45 degrees and rip a bevel with the outer face up for a tilt toward the fence or the inside face up for an outward tilt.

Rabbet Miter

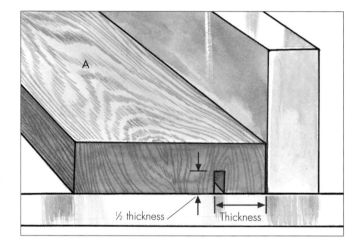

½ thickness — Thickness

1 Kerf the inside face with the distance between the fence and the outside of the blade equal to the wood thickness and the blade height set to half the thickness.

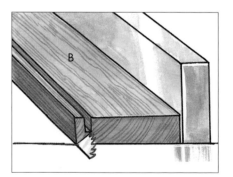

4 Flip the second part end for end so the inside is up and tilt the blade to remove the waste to the kerf at a 45-degree angle.

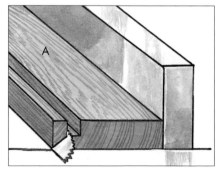

5 Flip the first part inside up and bevel its edge at the same 45-degree bevel angle, cutting to the groove left by kerfing out the waste.

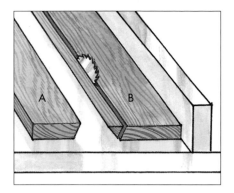

2 Flip the piece that is against the fence end for end and rip again to remove a triangular waste strip from the wood's edge.

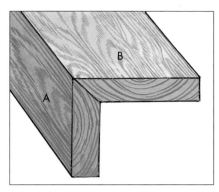

3 Flip the fence piece back again and join to the first piece for a near-perfect grain match.

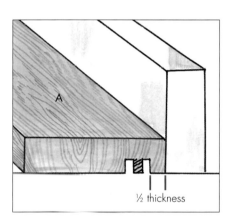

½ thickness

2 Move the fence so the distance to the blade's *inside* is half the wood thickness and kerf again, then move the fence to waste the material between the kerfs.

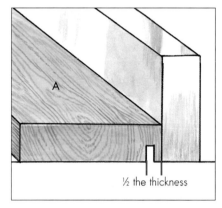

½ the thickness

3 Without changing the blade height, move the fence back so the distance to the blade outside is half the thickness and kerf the inside face of the second part.

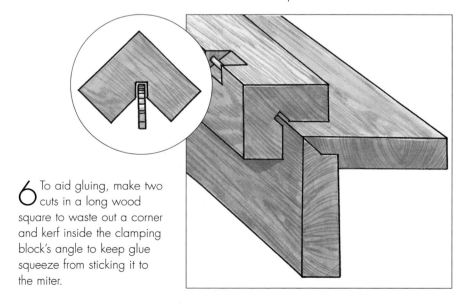

6 To aid gluing, make two cuts in a long wood square to waste out a corner and kerf inside the clamping block's angle to keep glue squeeze from sticking it to the miter.

Segmented constructions are easier to glue in pairs to make sure the bevel joint makes full contact along its entire length.

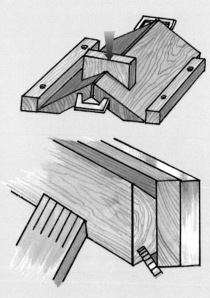

Groove bevels not 45 degrees using their cutting tilt for the blade angle setting and clamp down an angled fingerboard kerfed until it's flexible to hold the part vertical against the fence.

Coopering uses bevel-modified width joints to join segments of a circle's arc into one unit that is planed smooth of facets after the glue dries.

Compound Miters

Combining a miter angle with a blade tilt creates a compound miter. These miters tilt the sides of objects and stave constructions outward or inward. If the slope angle (the degree of tilt out or in) isn't critical, a "ballpark" miter angle and blade tilt will make an object that fits together. To make an object of an exact slope, height, and size takes a little more finesse.

A plan and elevation of any project should be drawn to work out problems before cutting begins. But neither view of a splayed object shows the actual shape of its parts or the actual miter and blade tilt angles.

Mathematicians can use trigonometry to calculate the blade tilt and bevel angle, but this chapter shows two drafted methods to devise the actual angles from the plan and elevation views. After this drafting work, it's simple to transfer the angles with a layout tool to the machine or to the lumber.

Compound miters are not impossible by hand, but they may not be practical with many sides or segments. The success of handmade compound miters depends on skill with a handplane.

The tablesaw or radial-arm saw make quick work of compound cutting once the set-up is tested in scraps. Like any miter, accuracy is critical. An error of one degree on each cut will multiply with the number of sides until the object won't fit together. One or two slight misalignments at glue-up will throw off the joinery.

A trick to correct errors comes from the process of gluing-up in pairs. After two parts are glued to make one unit, they are glued to another pair that have become one unit, then units are glued until the object is together. At any point during the glue-up, the angle between units can be checked against the plan and planed to correct any deviation.

The compound angles remain constant when the lengths of the sides vary like a square to a rectangle. When the slope angle varies between ends and sides, project each part's angle from the side and end elevations using the method shown at this chapter's beginning.

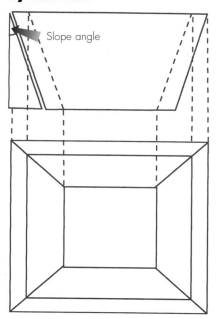

Slope angle

1 Draw a full-size elevation at the intended slope angle and develop a plan view of the piece.

Compound Miter by Hand

1 Use the drawing methods in this chapter to find the bevel angle, mark it on each end of a guide block and plane the edge to it.

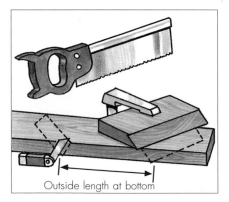

Outside length at bottom

2 Clamp the saw guide block across the inside of the part at the miter angle, making sure the bevel guides the saw cut toward the outside length of the part.

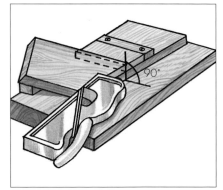

90°

3 On a shooting board, use double-stick tape to hold a tapered fence block that aligns the miter and a wood strip that tilts the bevel to 90 degrees and shave the miters to fit.

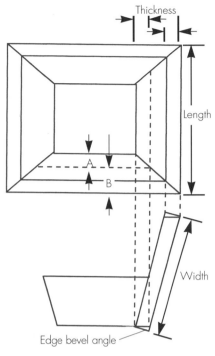

Thickness

Length

Width

A

B

Edge bevel angle

2 Drop perpendiculars from the plan and lay out the slope angle across them to find the actual part width and the edge bevel angle so the piece sits flat.

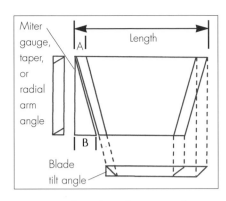

Miter gauge, taper, or radial arm angle

A

B

Length

Blade tilt angle

3 Project from the side view and use measurements A and B to lay out the miter angle, extending this angle's line and parallels to find the tilt angle.

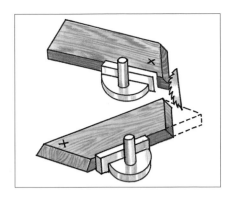

x

x

4 Set blade and gauge angles and miter one end of all parts, then tilt the gauge oppositely, turn the other edge to the gauge fence and cut to final length.

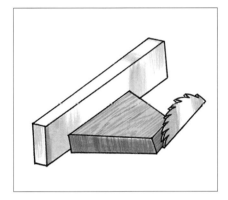

5 Cut the edge bevel on the top and bottom so the piece will sit flat, shifting the fence if necessary so the miter's point doesn't slip under it.

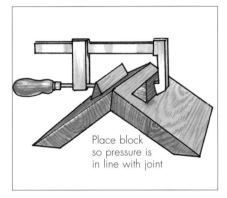

Place block so pressure is in line with joint

6 Temporarily glue bevelled strips on the parts with paper between for easy removal to direct the clamp force to the joint, then glue the piece in sections.

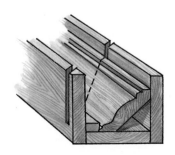

Coping and Mitering Molding

Outside corners must always be mitered, but inside corners can also be coped.

A molding that overhangs itself can only be mitered.

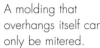

A molding that generally sweeps back can be coped.

To cope molding, bevel across the face to show the profile line, then cope saw along the profile vertically or slightly undercut and sand or file to fit.

To cut crown molding, mark the cabinet width on the molding bottom and align to the miter slot, propping the molding upside down and flat against the fence to cut the miter.

CHAPTER SEVEN

DOVETAILS

O ften considered the hallmark of fine workmanship in wood, dovetails are an interlocking joint with a great deal of mechanical strength. The joint is constructed with an angled male part shaped like the joint's name which fits into a similarly shaped female socket. In its best known configuration at an end to face corner, a dovetail joint is a series of tails fit into a series of sockets. The parts between sockets are called pins. They fit like interlocking tenons into the spaces between the tails. The widening tail braces the joint against tension, adding great mechanical strength to the long-grain glue surface between the tails and pins.

Choosing and Using Dovetails

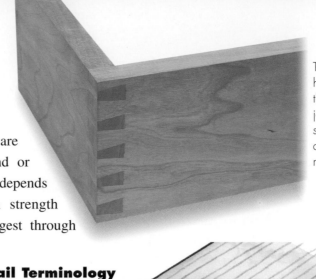

The three basic dovetail corner joints are through, half-blind or lapped, and blind or double lapped. The type of corner joint to use depends on the furniture style, and secondarily on strength requirements. In antique furniture, the strongest through dovetails (whose ends break through the board's face) were hidden under moldings. Half-blind or blind dovetails also kept the dovetail ends or entire joint from showing. Conversely, more contemporary designs will feature through dovetails on the carcass corners and drawers to advertise handcrafting. Modern adjustable dovetailing jigs imitate handwork, yielding variably spaced dovetails that subject this "handcrafted" look to scrutiny.

The dovetail shape transforms other joint families to strengthen them against tension. The sliding dovetail modifies a male tongue or tenon to fit a matching female housing. In the lap joint family, end laps reshaped as dovetails relieve tension on the glue bond, and even edge laps can include dovetailed shoulders that hold their unsupported end grain.

The dovetail modification of laps and sliding tongues and tenons has two forms: a single dovetail is barefaced with only one angled side and shoulder; a double dovetail has the full dovetail shape and usually includes a shoulder on each side.

Dovetail splines are used like loose tenons or regular splines to join wood. The butterfly key, named for its mirrored dovetail outline, and the dovetail key are decorative, functional reinforcing devices let into mating sockets.

Dovetail Terminology

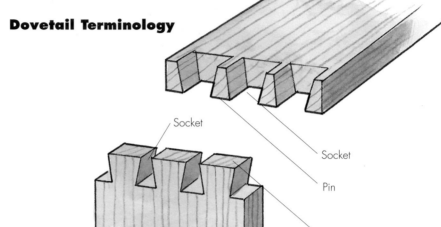

Socket

Socket

Pin

Tail

Basic Corner Dovetails

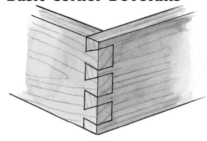

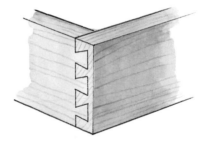

Through dovetails yield the largest glue surface possible in the joint but the ends of the boards show through on the mating faces.

Half-blind dovetails commonly hold a drawer face to the sides without letting the board ends show through on the drawer front.

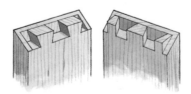

A blind mitered dovetail joint gives a corner joint hidden strength but allows the visual continuation of unbroken grain around the assembly.

On blind dovetails, the tails aren't cut through both faces like half-blind dovetails and either the pins or tails lap to keep any hint of dovetails from view.

Decorative Dovetail Reinforcements

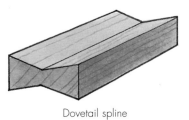

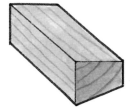

Dovetail spline   Butterfly key   Dovetail key

Dovetail splines, keys, or butterfly keys are used like regular splines or loose tenons to create or reinforce joints in several different families.

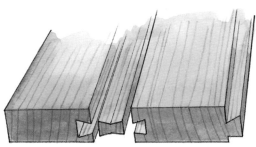
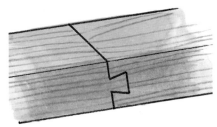

Form edge joints using dovetail splines or tongues with one or two shoulders, or reinforce and decorate them with butterfly keys.

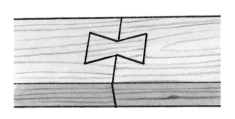
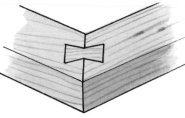

Several non-structural scarf joints are possible when the end to end joint is created by dovetails.

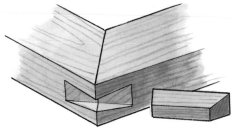
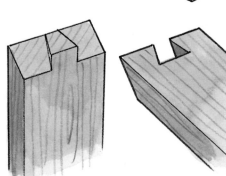

Decorative dovetail reinforcements assist the weak end grain glue bond of miter joints.

Modifying Joints with Dovetails

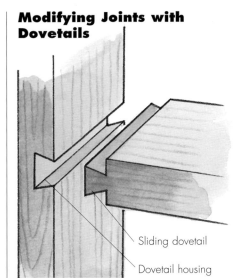

Sliding dovetail

Dovetail housing

A sliding dovetail extends the dovetail shape to modify a tongue or tenon that then must slide into its dovetail housing from the end.

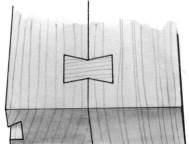
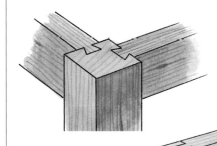

Dovetailing an open slot mortise and tenon corrects its weakness against downward force, and sliding dovetail tenons increase the rack resistance of a leg joint, stabilizing the structure.

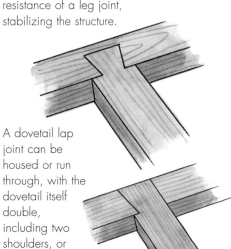

A dovetail lap joint can be housed or run through, with the dovetail itself double, including two shoulders, or single with one bare face.

Making Through Pins

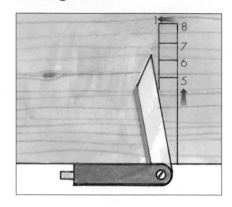

When developing a corner dovetail layout, make the pins about half the wood's thickness or more at their widest and evenly spaced tails about two or three times the pin width. Variable spacing uses wide tails at the center and narrower tails toward the joint's ends, setting out more pin gluing surface there but not necessarily proportioning the pins to either tail. This places strong construction where it's needed and helps restrain cupping if the wood dries. Layout should orient the heartwood side out to compensate for drying – drawers will bind if the sides cup outward.

1 Considering the type and species of wood, butt a sliding bevel to the bench edge and set the dovetail angle to a ratio between 1:5 and 1:8.

The half pins at each end of a corner dovetail joint aren't necessarily half the width of a whole pin. They are called half pins because only one side has the dovetail angle. Often they are made as wide at their widest end as a whole pin, or wider. Proper corner dovetails end with half pins to provide a gluing surface for the tail.

A ratio of less than 1:5 for the pin and tail angle makes the dovetail corners fragile, especially in coarse woods. The higher angle ratios flatten the wedge shape so are used for hardwoods less likely to shrink, or softwoods under little tension. Some pins on fine work narrow almost to points, but the width of the pin doesn't threaten joint strength like a tail that is too thin and weak at its narrowest part.

It's possible to saw pins on the tablesaw holding the part vertical against a scrap fence attached to a miter gauge. Angle the gauge until the blade cuts through the part at the pin angle, lowering the blade to the gauged line. Make all the cuts on one side of the pins in the waste, then turn the opposite face to make the other cuts.

On the scroll or bandsaw, the part is placed face down on the table and the end where the pins are marked is presented to the blade. The tilting saw table or a tilting auxiliary table aligns the pin angle to the blade.

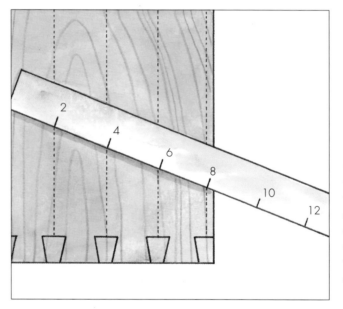

2 Design the layout on paper to develop the dovetail sizes; tilting a rule diagonally is an easy way to set equal increments for the pin centerlines and the spaces for mating tails.

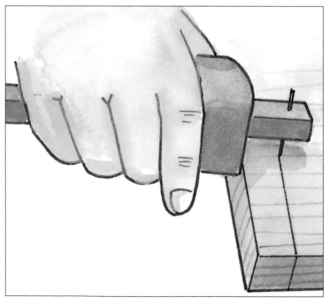

3 Dress and sand the wood, set the marking gauge just over the tail part's thickness and scribe around the end of the pin piece to mark its faces and edges.

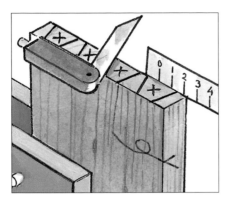

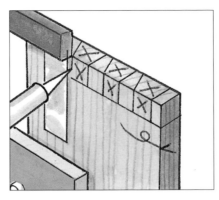

4 Facing the board's inside, lay out the pin centerlines, mark half the pin's widest end on each side of the centerline, scribe the angles with a knife, and mark the waste.

5 Square the pin angles down each face of the board to the gauged line with a knife and clearly mark the waste.

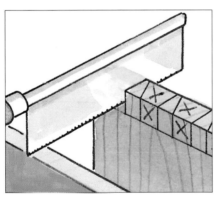

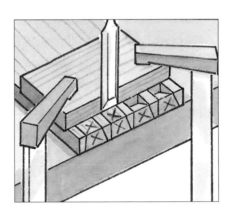

6 Starting at the front corner on the waste side of the pin lines, saw part way on the face and end, then level out to saw to the gauged line.

7 Clamp the part over a bench leg with a guide block on the gauged line, chop down at the line and chisel away half the waste, angling down from the end grain.

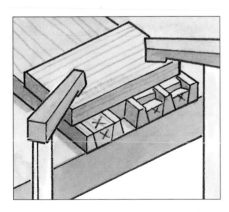

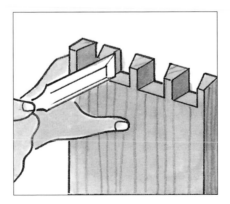

8 Flip the part and chop away the remaining waste with small steps that move back toward the gauged line and down into the waste until all the waste is removed.

9 Clean up inside the pins, making sure to keep the cheeks flat and perpendicular and pare the end grain flat or undercut to a slight V indent.

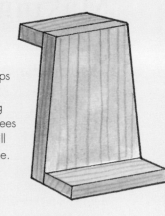

A piece of scrap cut at the dovetail angle with attached stops at each end aids marking and guarantees the angle will stay the same.

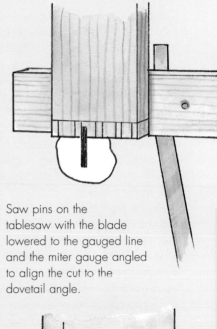

Saw pins on the tablesaw with the blade lowered to the gauged line and the miter gauge angled to align the cut to the dovetail angle.

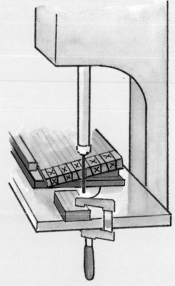

To saw pins on the bandsaw, tilt the bandsaw table itself or make a tilted jig, using a clamped block to stop the cut at the gauged line.

Making Through Tails

To mark the tails from the pins, gauge the pin stock thickness around the end of the tail board and butt the pin board to the line in the assembled position, clamping if necessary. Scribe the sides of the pins onto the inside face of the tail board from the inside face of the pins so the knife doesn't follow the grain away.

As with any handsawing, small bevels can be chiseled into the waste of the end grain layout or a shallow kerf can be made along the line to guide the saw. Tilt the board to make the cuts vertical if it gives better control. A first light cut at the back corner is another technique to keep the saw aligned.

To saw tails on the tablesaw, tilt the blade to the tail angle and hold the part vertical against a squared miter gauge. First cut the same side of each tail, then reverse the board faces to cut the other side. Alternatively, carefully bandsaw the cuts with the board face flat on the table.

Setting the marking gauge slightly over the thickness makes the joint ends proud, to be sanded flush after glue-up. Many woodworkers prefer this option to gauging slightly under the thickness, which leaves the ends recessed in their sockets and requires planing or sanding down the whole face of the board. In the case of a fitted drawer, the final width is the critical issue. It's a matter of preference whether the drawer face is cut overlong to compensate for sanding down proud ends to fit, or cut to exact size and the sides planed down to the recessed ends to fit.

Choosing to leave the ends proud complicates clamping. The proud ends prevent clamps from pushing the dovetails into the sockets by direct pressure unless comb-like clamping blocks are used to press between the ends. However, since the glue surface is between the tails and pins, the important force should be against the width of the joint after other clamps seat the parts. Some feel tight dovetails needn't be clamped, just left undisturbed until the glue dries.

1 Set the marking gauge slightly over the thickness of the pin stock and scribe around the end of the tail stock after it has been dressed, squared, and sanded.

2 Hold or clamp the widest side of the cut pins to the gauged line on the tails, scribing inside the sockets to mark the pin positions inside the tail stock.

3 Square the scribed pin angle lines across the end of the board and mark the pin positions as waste.

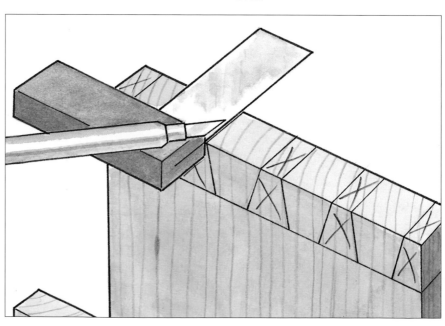

4 Saw on the waste side of the pin angles, starting on the front corner to saw face and end simultaneously, tilting the board to make the cuts vertical if preferred.

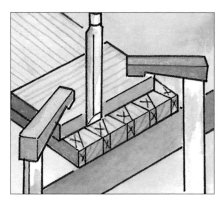

5 One method chops out the waste with a narrow chisel using the same process as with the pins, tilting the chisel slightly if undercut end grain is desired.

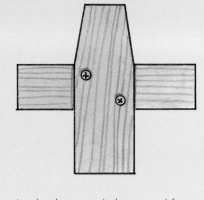

Another homemade layout tool for dovetails can set the angle for the tails and pins, as well as square the lines across the end grain and down the face.

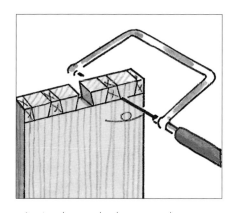

6 Another method removes the waste by sawing near the line, then paring the end grain flush to the gauged line.

7 Clean up the sockets between the tails, using if necessary special skew or dovetail chisels with angled edges that can reach under the overhang of the tail.

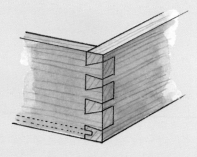

The layout of through dovetails on drawers lets the bottom groove run out under a tail and through a pin where the open groove on the drawer's side is plugged.

8 Protect the joint with a block and tap it together, making sure that the pins and tails align to their sockets and that their wide ends aren't too tight and cause splits.

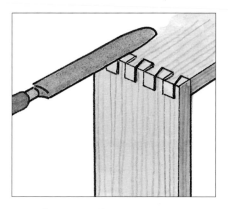

9 After gluing, file or use a block to sand flush the slightly raised pins and tails caused by gauging the line a little over the thickness of the stock.

A corner miter dovetail layout insets the half pin from the edge, but one face line of the half pin isn't sawn, and the extra material beyond it is mitered.

Making Lapped Dovetails

The three basic lapped dovetails are half-blind, blind mitered, and full-blind. The biggest difference from through dovetails is that lapped dovetails help to hide all or part of the joint to serve design.

A dovetailing preference that is brought into focus by the lap family is whether the pins or the tails should be made first. The method shown for through dovetails makes the pins first and scribes the tails from them. Some woodworkers prefer to work the other way around. In practice, the length of the parts decides the order because one is easier to align to the other for scribing. Dovetails in the lap family can be made either way, but blind mitered and full-blinds with the lap on the tails can't be made tails first because scribing is awkward or impossible.

Half-blind dovetails use two gauge settings for layout regardless of part thickness, while through dovetails can use the same setting for all gauging unless part thickness differs. When laying out half-blinds, the scribe on the end grain not only sets the length of the tails but it establishes the joint's strength based on glue surface and mechanical resistance. Never under-scribe this dimension onto the tails part or misalign the tails to it for scribing or the joint won't fit tight.

Initially, the tail and pin parts of blind mitered dovetails are laid out the same. Equally thick parts are rabbeted from the inside face about ⅔ the thickness toward the opposite face and about ⅓ the distance down to the inside scribed line. The rabbet width and depth should intersect at a point along the 45-degree shoulder line scribed on the part's edge. Then the pins are laid out on the rabbet like a mitered corner dovetail, and the tails are scribed from them.

Full-blind dovetails let the pins or tails carry the lap so the joint can be oriented against tension and still hidden. The layout determines whether the end grain section shows on the side or top. The sidebar drawing shows the tails carrying the lap as they would to keep a weight-bearing cabinet side absent of visible joinery.

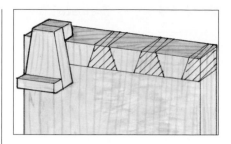

3 Determine the layout spacing and sizes and use a template or sliding bevel to scribe angles for the tails on the side's outside face, then square the lines across the end.

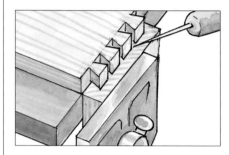

4 After sawing and chiseling the tails, hold the parts in assembly position with the tails exactly on the front's end grain scribe line in order to scribe them onto the front's end.

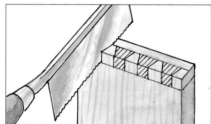
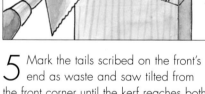

5 Mark the tails scribed on the front's end as waste and saw tilted from the front corner until the kerf reaches both scribed lines but doesn't go past them.

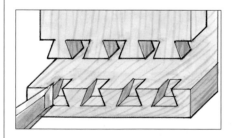

6 Chop down into the waste and chip it out from the end grain, guide the chisel against the pin side to reach the unsawn inside corners, then test fit the joint.

Half-Blind Dovetails

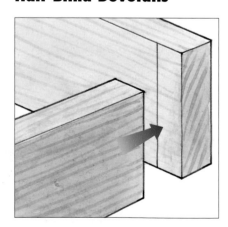

1 Using a drawer as the example, square and sand the stock, set the marking gauge to the side's thickness, and then scribe it on the inside face of the front.

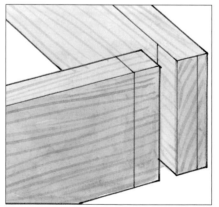

2 Reset the gauge to scribe about ⅔ the thickness of the front on its end grain and also around the end of the side on both the faces and edges.

Blind Mitered Dovetails

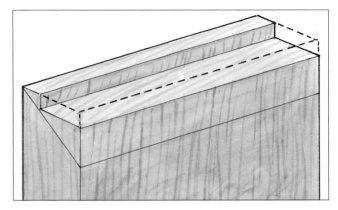

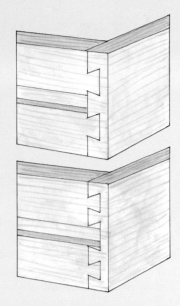

1 Scribe the exact thickness inside each part, connect a 45-degree scribe from each edge, then rabbet about ⅓ toward the face scribe but not past the angled line.

When using half-blind dovetails, lay out the runner groove of side-hung drawers so it uses the drawer front as a stop.

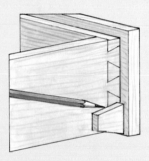

For a lipped drawer, the sides are dovetailed into the rabbet cut around the edge of the drawer front, and pins are marked from a template or from tails made first.

2 Lay out the pins with a template, leaving material past the half pin as in mitered corner dovetails, clear the sockets, then saw the edge's mitered shoulder, and finally miter the end lip.

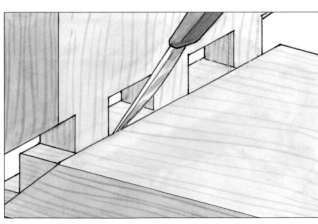

3 Place the pin part in position on the tail part against the scribed line, scribe the tails, remove the socket waste, and cut the mitered shoulder and mitered end.

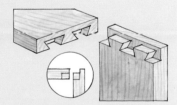

Full-blind dovetails are similar to half-blind and blind mitered dovetails, with either the pins or tails carrying the lap and the layout keeping the joint hidden.

Sliding Dovetails

The sliding dovetail is a modification that mechanically reinforces certain tongues or tenons against tension. The oldest hand-cut versions like the tapered sliding dovetail, a housing joint, are being replaced by routed versions, often without the taper. These have the liability of being more difficult to slide over a length than the tapered version, which begins to tighten only as the last few inches are slid home.

Some classic designs used the sliding dovetail to join the drawer sides and back. The sides traditionally extended past the back to keep the drawer from falling out when fully open, so the sliding dovetail wasn't weakened with a housing too close to the end, creating weak short grain. The dovetail held the sides in against the weight of bulging contents and the forces of drying wood. As a joint between drawer fronts and sides, the drawer front layout needs a lip at each end so that the single or double dovetail housing run in it isn't weakened by short grain.

Any sliding dovetail housing (sometimes questionably called dovetail mortises), can be stopped so the dovetail shape of the tenon or tongue doesn't break through the edge and the joint remains hidden. When machining the housings, groove or dado through the material to waste most of it, then make the final trimming cut with the dovetail router bit to save wear and tear on the bit, motor, and material.

There are as many methods for routing sliding dovetails as there are woodworkers, but no matter how the joint is made material flatness affects accurate milling and in turn the ease of assembly. The adjustable horizontal jig shown has the advantage of referencing the material off the same face when routing double dovetails and canceling the effects of any cupping in the board.

Clamps help pull together long sliding dovetails, which, when used on shelving, needn't be glued their full length. Gluing at the front edge to hold the part in position is usually enough and saves struggling in assembly with an obstinate joint swollen with glue.

Stopped Tapered Dovetail by Hand

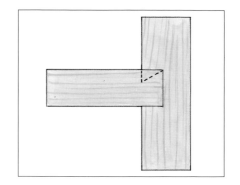

1 Match a dovetail angle to the dovetail saw and plane, then determine the width of dovetail that will fit within the stock thickness, leaving a small shoulder.

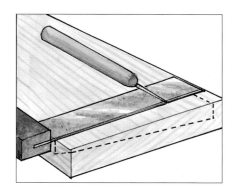

4 Scribe the dovetail depth square across the shelf face, mark the dovetail profile on the back edge, then mark the same taper angle across the end as the housing.

Sliding Dovetail Drawer Joint

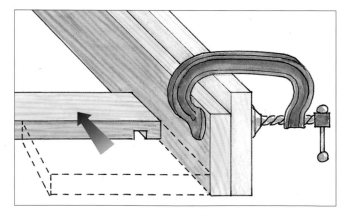

1 On a router table with an auxiliary wooden fence, steady the part with a plywood square and use a straight bit to waste a groove about half the material's depth.

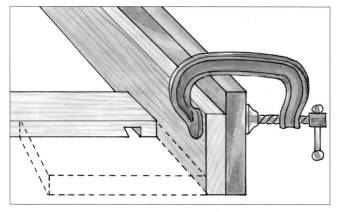

2 For a single shoulder dovetail, change to a dovetail bit and cut the angled shoulder without the bit touching the straight outside shoulder of the groove.

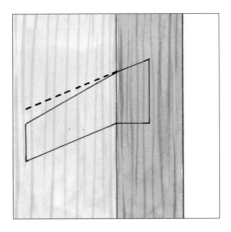

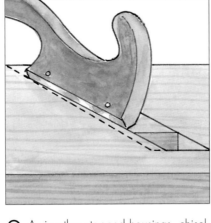

2 Lay out the dovetail width at less than half the thickness of the housing part's back edge and square lines across, but taper the top line narrower toward the front.

3 As in other stopped housings, chisel a hole to allow sawing, saw the straight shoulder to the correct depth, then use the angled dovetail saw to cut the dovetail shoulder.

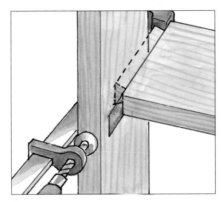

5 Use the dovetail plane to remove the shoulder material and taper the dovetail tongue to the marked end grain line.

6 Trim the tongue to the stop and test slide it into the housing, where it will be loose until the last when a clamp can pull it tight.

3 Without changing the bit height, slide the fence over so only part of the bit shaves the tongue on the end of drawer side until it fits the dovetail housing.

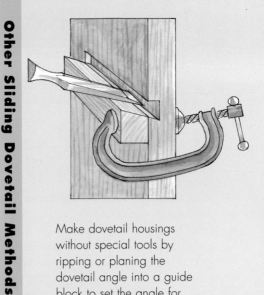

Make dovetail housings without special tools by ripping or planing the dovetail angle into a guide block to set the angle for chiseling and sawing the housing and tongue.

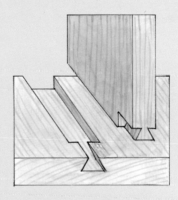

A routed version of a dovetailed housing uses a saddle jig to guide a dado, then changes to a dovetail bit to dovetail the housing's front end through or stopped.

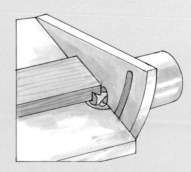

Rout tongues horizontally with the router mounted on a pivoting fence, which is locked by a knob to the table's edge so the bit can be raised to cut a second shoulder.

Dovetail Keys, Splines, and Butterflies

The dovetail shape in the form of keys, splines, and butterfly keys is popular and effective as a decorative reinforcement. The butterfly key has even become the signature reinforcement of certain craft movements and craft builders.

For strength, dovetail keys are cut with the grain. One use creates mock dovetails that reinforce corner miter joints. Keys can be of a contrasting wood but even the same species yields a color change because the trimmed key shows all end grain.

The sliding dovetail batten is a utilitarian key, made wide and fit unglued into a dovetail housing on one side of slab glue-ups such as tabletops or doors. These battens allow the wood to move but keep the assembly flat.

The least common dovetail spline is just as easy (or difficult) to fit as a machined sliding dovetail. The housings are simple, but fitting the dovetail to it requires a lot of testing in scrap. Once the machine set-up of the router or tablesaw is fine tuned, running the splines is easy. As with other splines, the grain runs across the width of dovetail splines for strength. If cut on the tablesaw, the V in the center of the spline might need some clean-up with a chisel or rabbet plane.

Butterfly keys are made so the grain runs parallel to the length of their face. Set in across the grain, they create a minor dimensional conflict to consider when designing their length. Their thickness can vary in proportion to the ground wood, the wood into which they're set. One famous English craftsman made them the same thickness and cut the recesses through to show them on both sides of the tabletops they were reinforcing.

Dark wood butterfly key

To save chiseling recesses, make a router template in two parts for easy access to sawing the shape. Medium density fiberboard or MDF, a fine-grain particle board in different thicknesses, makes excellent template material. An overbearing flush trim bit eliminates the calculation of template guide offsets so the template can be cut from the scribed size of the key. The router leaves round corners to chisel out of the recess, or the key corners can be rounded instead.

Dovetail Keys

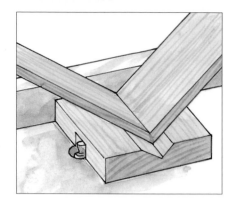

1 Rout dovetail housings in mitered corners using a V-block with a through dado for bit passage and turning the frame to cut each corner.

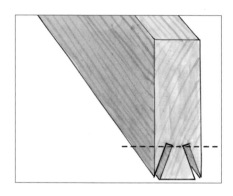

2 Set the tablesaw blade to the dovetail angle and make two kerfs in the edge with the grain in order to create a matching dovetail shape, then rip off the key.

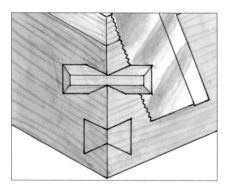

3 Tap short lengths of key material into the dovetail housings with glue, trim off with a saw once dry, and sand.

Dovetail Splines

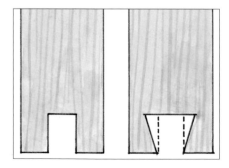

1 On a router table or tablesaw, make a groove to waste some of the material, then rout with a dovetail bit to form the dovetail housing.

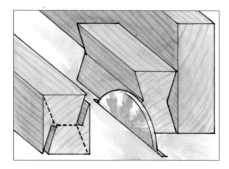

2 Lay out dovetails on a board's edge to match the housing and adjust the sawblade angle and depth. Then cut the first two angles, rotate end for end, and cut the others.

Butterfly Keys

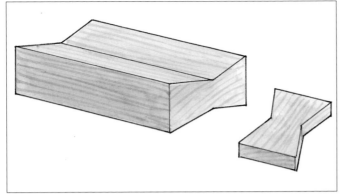

1 Make a length of dovetail spline, then cut butterfly key inlays like bread slices about ⅓ the stock thickness being inlaid plus extra to plane flush after gluing.

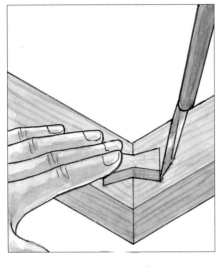

2 Hold or clamp the reinforcing inlay in place across the joint and scribe around it, tilting the knife handle away from the inlay so the tip bevels in toward it.

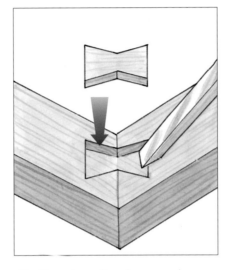

3 Chop the outline deeper and leverage the waste with the chisel's bevel side down, glue in the inlay, beveling its entry edge if necessary and plane flush when dry.

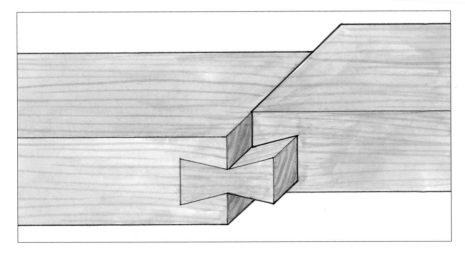

3 Test the spline's fit, thinning it slightly with a rabbet plane or sanding block if it's too tight, then tap the parts together or pull together with a clamp.

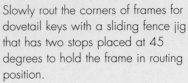

Slowly rout the corners of frames for dovetail keys with a sliding fence jig that has two stops placed at 45 degrees to hold the frame in routing position.

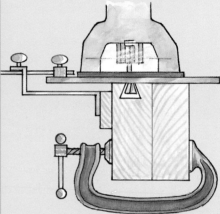

Rout dovetail housings or even tongues in edges and ends by clamping on extra material to support the router and aligning the cut with the router edge guide.

Butt two pieces of template material, outline a butterfly key, separate them to saw interior angles, then glue together to guide an overbearing flush trim bit to rout the recess.

CHAPTER EIGHT

DOWELS
AND BISCUITS

Modernized versions of common joints have developed over time to speed manufacturing or accommodate new materials. Dowel joints and biscuit joinery are both by-products of industry. They make quick work of joinery by eliminating time-consuming fitting of joined elements, and are alternatives that should find an appropriate place in every woodworker's repertoire.

About Dowels

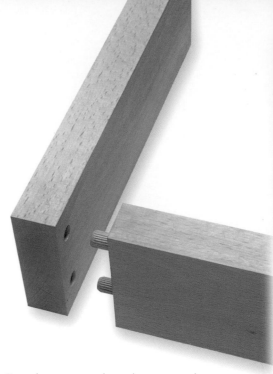

Dowels, also called dowel pins, are cylindrical bits of wood that form a joint when glued like loose tenons into aligning holes drilled in two wood parts. Their three basic functions in joinery are to substitute for tenons and tongues, or to reinforce or to align joints.

Commercial dowels matched to standard drill sizes

10 mm   8 mm   6 mm

Doweling is a simple and economical way to reinforce a light duty butted corner joint.

Commercial birch or maple dowels come in standard diameters from ¼" to ½" and several lengths. Alternatively dowels can be made in the shop from lengths of dowel rod. Chamfered dowel ends ease insertion and keep dowels from burring over when they're tapped home. Tapping in the dowel can create a piston effect, compressing air and glue in the hole. This hydraulic pressure makes assembly difficult and could split the part. So spiral or straight flutes are cut in the dowels to relieve the pressure. In use, dowel diameter should be ⅓ to ½ the part thickness. Holes in each part should be drilled to a minimum depth 1½ times the diameter. Holes should be countersunk to collect escaping glue.

Commercial dowels matched to standard drill sizes must be kept dry so they don't swell with moisture. Swollen dowels can be dried in an oven prior to use. Shopmade dowels are cut from doweling rod that is sized by driving it through a dowel plate, a piece of mild steel drilled with the appropriate size hole, and countersunk

on the exiting side. The rod can be fluted and cut to lengths or each cut length can be fluted and chamfered for insertion.

The quality and durability of dowel joints are widely debated. While they might not substitute for dovetails in a carpenter's portable toolbox, dowels in a wall-hung cabinet have the same chance as any other joint to endure the stresses of wood movement on the glue bond while creating some extra flexibility in design.

Because dowels are wood they are subject to the same effects of wood movement on length and width as any other wood part. Depending on grain orientation, a dowel joint will be strong and free from dimensional conflict, or it will have little long-grain contact for gluing, lots of conflict, and be weak against tension and glue shear.

Types of Dowels

Commercial spiral-fluted dowels allow excess glue and air to escape from the hole, avoiding hydraulic pressure as the joint is assembled. Straight-fluted commercial dowels don't scrape all the glue off the sides of the hole and are easy to insert, but they are not as readily available.

Dowelmaking in the Shop

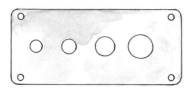

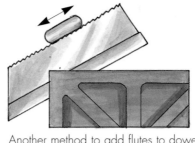

Dowel rod is sized by driving it through holes in a steel dowel plate or pop; holes in commercial versions are sometimes toothed inside to simultaneously cut flutes.

Another method to add flutes to dowels cut from rod is to run them along a sawblade to form one or two glue channels.

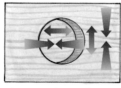

A cheap and effective fluter can be made from scrapwood with a hole that fits a dowel rod; screw or nail points protruding into the hole cut the flutes.

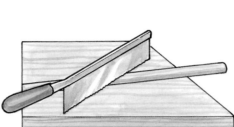

Some woodworkers roll dowel rod with a saw held on the diagonal to make teeth marks that hold dried glue like flutes, theorizing it mechanically reinforces the glue bond.

A dowel pointer chucks into a drill or brace and works like a pencil sharpener to chamfer dowel ends; alternatively, they could be twirled against a belt or disk sander.

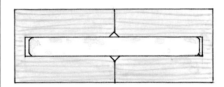

Taking Care in Doweling

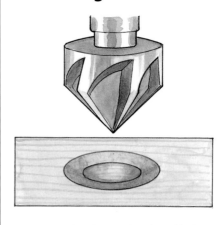

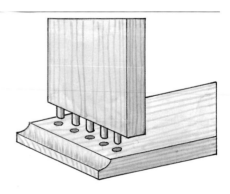

A countersink enlarges the dowel hole, making a reservoir to contain escaping glue that would otherwise ooze out of the joint onto the wood surface.

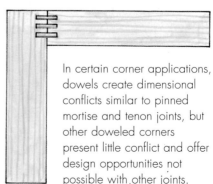

Dowel holes should be drilled a minimum of 1½ times the diameter in each part with a slight glue reservoir at the bottom and at the countersunk edge.

Dowels and Wood Movement

In the worst grain orientation, a dowel will shrink away from the mostly end grain glue surface in its hole and subject the joint to racking.

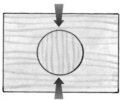

Even inserted in the best orientation, where the dowel moves in the same direction as the part's wood, a dowel has only two tiny points of long-grain contact with its hole.

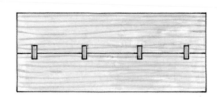

The long grain of dowels in width joints creates dimensional conflict against width movement; dowels should be cut under length and spaced widely if used for parts alignment in such situations.

In a length joint, the long grain of dowels runs parallel to that of the parts, so there is no conflict.

In certain corner applications, dowels create dimensional conflicts similar to pinned mortise and tenon joints, but other doweled corners present little conflict and offer design opportunities not possible with other joints.

Using Dowels

It makes sense to build with dowels when joinery isn't a design feature and tension on the joint won't be in line with the dowels. Doweled parts usually butt together, so doweling simplifies cutting parts to length with no extending tenons to calculate. Doweling requires only that the parts meet squarely and the holes align straight. However, hole placement must be accurate to within the thickness of a few sheets of paper.

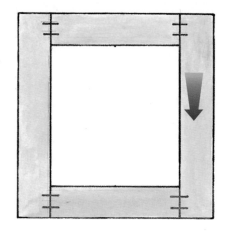

Dowels used in a door frame are strong against shearing but not a good choice in a drawer face where tension pulls in line with the dowels.

A number of proprietary doweling jigs on the market aid accurate drilling. Their features and abilities vary, but their main function is to carry a bushing that fits the drill bit and guides it 90 degrees to the wood surface. Such jigs usually locate holes along a line.

A row of holes for dowels is laid out along the *x* plane, usually a board's edge or end. The thickness of the edge is then the *y* plane. Commercial jigs locate the hole within the *y* plane by automatically centering it or by referencing from one face of the board while an adjustment sets the hole's *y*-plane location.

Jigs have index marks to set the bushing center at hole locations marked along the *x* plane. Mating hole locations are transferred to the mating part during layout by squaring marks across the edge or by markers called dowel centers, which are used after drilling the first part. Some jigs position the bushing to drill a mating hole by indexing from a dowel inserted in the first hole. Others hold parts in alignment to drill mating holes in pairs. Few commercial jigs allow for drilling in a board's face or for more than one or two holes at a time, so shopmade jigs are more adaptable and efficient for carcass joinery.

A steady hand can make a simple through dowel joint by freehand drilling into both parts while they're clamped in assembly position. The dowel ends that show at the surface can be kerfed and wedged, plugged, or covered by moldings. Some doweling is possible on the drill press, but it's often easier to use its accuracy to drill a scrap block of dense wood for a single-use jig to guide a hand-held drill.

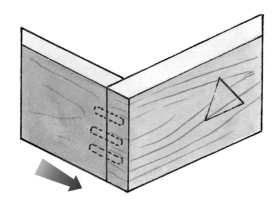

Dowel Hole Accuracy

Holes not 90 degrees

Both dowel holes must be drilled 90 degrees to the wood surface so the dowel will seat; for good alignment dowels should be referenced from the same face or centered.

Holes accidentally referenced from opposite faces

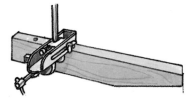

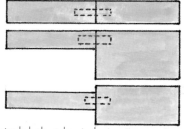

A single-hole edge indexing jig carrying interchangeable bushings registers from the same face of both parts and will align them flush unless the registration is readjusted to create an offset.

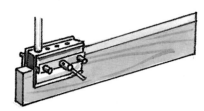

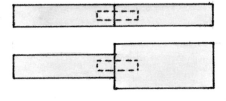

A self-centering jig with integral bushings drills only in the center of the board's edge and won't align the faces of different sized stock.

Laying Out and Transferring Hole Positions

The hole spacing is marked out along the *x* plane and squared across to a mating part while jigs or machines are set to repeat the *y* location.

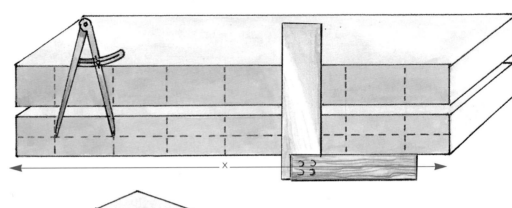

Some jigs index the mating hole from a dowel inserted in the first hole, while others position the parts to drill mating holes at the same time.

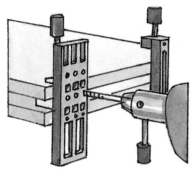

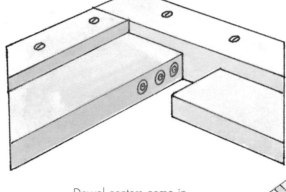

Dowel centers come in different hole sizes and work best to mark the drilling locations in mating parts if a temporary frame is used to guide the parts into position.

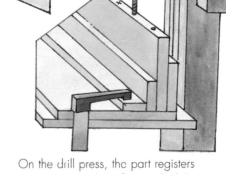

On the drill press, the part registers against an auxiliary fence which locates and repeats the *y* location of the dowel holes spaced out along the *x* plane.

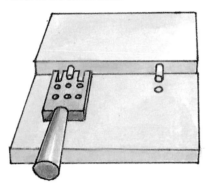

Shopmade doweling jigs

To compensate for any deviation from 90 degrees in a shopmade jig's holes, always drill mating parts from the opposite jig side by jig design or by reversing the fence.

A simple self-centering jig could be adapted like any shop jig to carry some types of commercial steel drill bushings sold as spares.

Single-use hardwood jigs made on the drill press can be laid out with any number of holes, reference from any face, and held in place by brads or clamps.

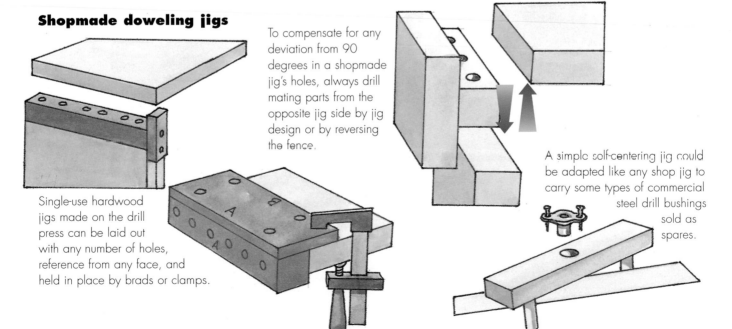

Making Dowel Joints

The doweling method is determined by where the holes are needed in the parts and the easiest available tool to drill them accurately. Board edges are easy to drill on the drill press, but the ends of long cabinet sides are better suited to a portable drill and jig.

Regardless of the tools used, the basic procedure for doweling is the same. First, choose a dowel diameter and matching drill bit ⅓ to ½ the stock thickness. Then, cut the stock to size and mark a centered or offset hole location within the y plane of one part's thickness. For a shopmade jig, do this layout on stock matched to the parts.

Next, extend a line paralleling the x plane from the marked y point and lay out a row of holes along it, spacing the dowels according to their purpose of aligning, reinforcing, or substituting for mortise and tenon. Dowels for alignment are minimal; as tenons, they should be placed closer together but at least a diameter apart so the hole walls aren't weak.

The next step varies to fit the method for transferring the hole locations to mating parts. For a single-hole doweling jig or drill press, square the marks across to all the parts. For jigs that index off an inserted dowel, or jigs that align mating parts for simultaneous drilling, mark only the first set of holes for dowel centers. A shopmade jig carries the entire layout and eliminates marking.

Used as tenons, dowels should enter each mating part to a minimum depth 1½ times the dowel diameter. Used for alignment, dowels can be shorter. Set a bit depth stop or the drill press to drill the hole deep enough for the dowel plus a slight glue reservoir.

Use the drill press or index the jig on the marks to drill the holes. Put the bit into the jig hole or bushing before starting to drill, occasionally backing the running drill bit partly out of the hole to clear the flutes. Don't press down hard when nearing the stop or it could slip up the shank of the bit.

Drill Bits and Stops

The right drill bit determines the success of a doweled joint. A bit has to be capable of positive location and stay on course in both end and face grain. Secondary considerations are preventing tear-out in face grain and whether the bit leaves an easy-to-measure flat-bottomed hole.

Heat build-up in the holes during drilling can cause the bit to lose temper and dull easily so the wood cells don't cut cleanly. If the bit gets too hot, chemical residues are created on the wood surface. Both these conditions affect the glue bond. The bit's ability to pull wood chips away from the cutting edge is critical to reducing heat build-up. The operator can help promote cooling by occasionally backing the running bit partly out of the hole to clear it.

Drill bits that meet these criteria are brad point bits, Forstner or multi-spur bits for the drill press, and Jennings or Irwin pattern bits for the brace. Twist drills can be used for doweling, but the bit will shred face grain and may not center easily. A detent punched at the mark provides a little starting guidance.

To gauge the dowel hole depth on a portable drill or brace, a depth stop is put on the bit. Stops are as simple as a piece of masking tape with an extending tab that sweeps the surface when the drill reaches the right depth to commercial steel collars held on by set screws. A Fuller countersink and stop on a bit in the drill press will drill the hole to the right depth and countersink a glue reservoir, all in one operation.

Reinforced Width Miter

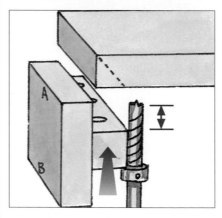

1 Cut the parts to final length, make a jig for drilling inside the miter, set the stop to drill the chosen depth, and tap on the jig with brads.

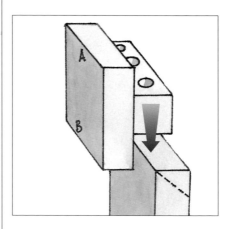

2 Drill the mating holes in the second part from the opposite side of the jig, then saw the miter across all the parts without removing any length.

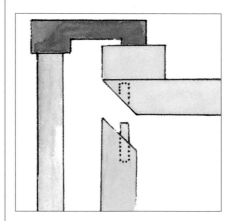

3 Brush glue in the holes and on the dowels, inserting them in one part and using a block to close the miter's edge while clamping down on the dowels.

Molded Edge Carcass Joint

1 Cut the part to be molded to length and width, then map out the molding and side placement to make a jig, spacing the holes closer together near the edges.

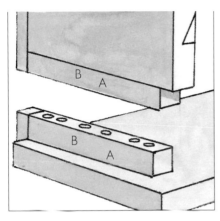

2 Drill the carcass parts, making sure to index the jig from the same face and reverse the fence to drill mating parts from the opposite side of the jig.

3 Cut the molding, brush glue in the holes and tap in the dowels, using a height block to stop them just short of the hole bottom to leave a glue reservoir.

Doweled Framing Joint

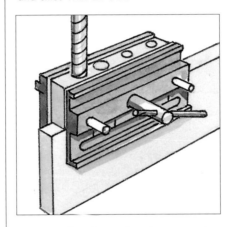

1 Make a layout template that substitutes dowels and holes at the mortise and tenon position, then mark the dowel hole positions on rails and stiles with an awl.

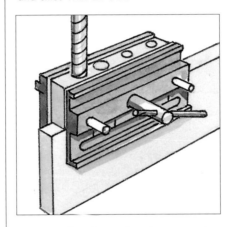

2 To drill, index a doweling jig to the awl marks, inserting a shim against the wood's face if necessary to adjust the holes off the center of the y plane.

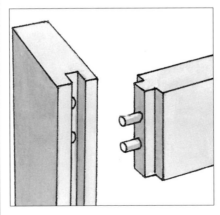

3 Complete any remaining milling on the frame, whether grooves, rabbets, moldings, or haunches, glue in the dowels, and assemble.

Brad point

Forstner

Multi-spur

Jennings pattern

Irwin pattern

Wood stop collar

Fuller countersink and stop collar

About Biscuit Joinery

Biscuit or plate joining is a relatively new method for joining wood. It was developed to join manmade materials like plywood and particle board, but it has also become popular for joining solid wood.

Biscuits are thin, football-shaped pieces of compressed beech that join parts like loose tenons, dowels, or splines. Most biscuit joints are made by a portable electric tool called a plate joiner, which looks like a small right angle grinder with a carbide-toothed sawblade. The machine's main function is to plunge its blade to a calibrated depth into mating parts. Each semi-circular kerf left in the parts by the blade encloses half the biscuit.

A biscuit joint is quickly made by a devoted hand power tool.

About Biscuit Joiners

The retractable spring-loaded base of the plate joiner encloses a small circular sawblade that is plunged into the wood to various depth settings, making arced kerfs that fit the biscuits.

Biscuits themselves are made from compressed beech cut so the grain runs diagonally across them for strength. There are three standard sizes used by all machines (0, 10, 20) and certain machines can use larger biscuits or kerf for smaller, thinner biscuits using a non-standard blade. Spline cutters used in routers or laminate trimmers can rout kerfs for special round biscuits.

Biscuits require water-based glues like aliphatic resins. By design, the moisture swells the slightly compressed biscuit, tightening it in the kerf. Biscuit joints perform extremely well in strength tests.

The number of plate joiners on the market offers woodworkers a choice of features over an extended price range. Important considerations are the ease and range of fence adjustment, the range of fence angles, and the miter indexing method.

Most biscuit joinery references the machine's fence against the wood's face or end to position the kerf. The distance between the blade and the fence has some adjustment. The most versatile blade height adjustment uses a rack and pinion to move the fence up and down in relation to the blade, although in practice an infinite number of positions aren't often needed given common wood thicknesses.

On all machines the fence references at 90 degrees to the surface being kerfed to make most parallel, T, or L joints, and at 45 degrees for end or edge miters. Some fences also reference at any angle in between, a handy feature for joining beveled work. The machine also references off its flat base.

A less common type of biscuit joiner doubles as a panel saw and the motor housing pivots on the base to plunge the side-emerging blade into the wood.

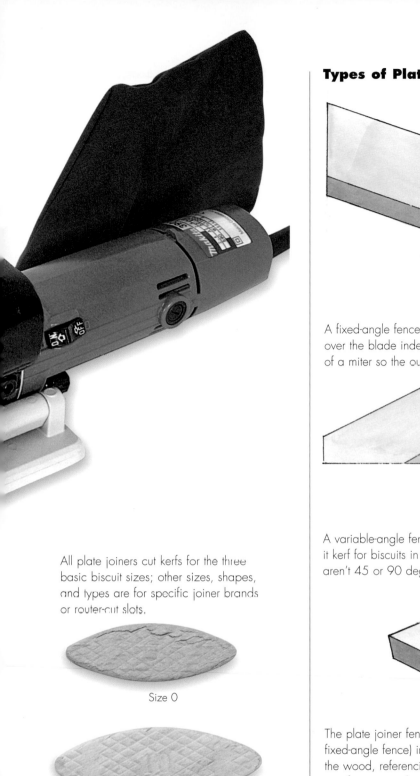

All plate joiners cut kerfs for the three basic biscuit sizes; other sizes, shapes, and types are for specific joiner brands or router-cut slots.

Size 0

Size 10

Size 20

Types of Plate Joiner Fences

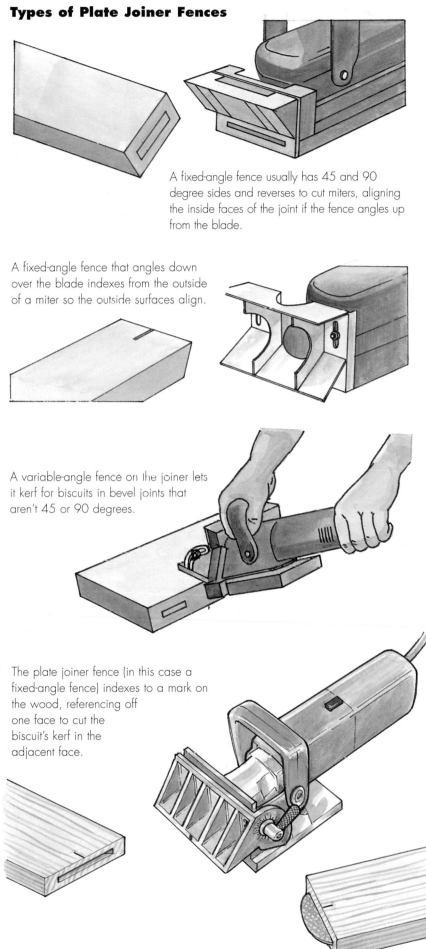

A fixed-angle fence usually has 45 and 90 degree sides and reverses to cut miters, aligning the inside faces of the joint if the fence angles up from the blade.

A fixed-angle fence that angles down over the blade indexes from the outside of a miter so the outside surfaces align.

A variable-angle fence on the joiner lets it kerf for biscuits in bevel joints that aren't 45 or 90 degrees.

The plate joiner fence (in this case a fixed-angle fence) indexes to a mark on the wood, referencing off one face to cut the biscuit's kerf in the adjacent face.

Making Biscuit Joints

Biscuits joints are so simple to make it's not surprising they've become popular. The layout doesn't require precision, machine set-up is simple, and the joint is cut in seconds. In addition, biscuit machines are very safe. The base or the wood always encloses the blade and retractable pins or rubber spots on the base resist slippage during kerfing.

The basic biscuit joining procedure is the same regardless of the type of joint. Cut the parts to size and clamp or hold them in assembly position to mark the location of each biscuit across the joint with a soft pencil. Since biscuits have a little side-to-side play in the kerf for joint adjustment during glue-up, marking doesn't have to be precise.

The biscuit size to use and layout spacing depends on the wood's dimensions and the purpose of the joint. Wood thickness has to be more than half the biscuit width for kerfs into the face or the blade will come through the back face. When one biscuit runs across a part's end as in frame joints, the length of the biscuit shouldn't exceed the part's width or the biscuit will show on the edges. More or bigger biscuits give more glue surface for increased strength, but aren't necessary if the biscuits are there only for alignment. As usual, wood movement issues apply to biscuited joints.

Whether the joint is marked across its inside or outside depends on the type of joint and the referencing method being used: either the straight or angled fence or the base of the machine. Initial marks can be squared around or extended so the machine's index mark is easy to line up to them during kerfing.

Clamp down parts for kerfing or set up a backstop to keep them from sliding back when the blade is pushed into the wood. Dust usually ejects to the right, so start on the right and move left to keep referencing surfaces clean if the machine does not have dust collection. Special expensive glue bottles are available to apply glue to the kerfs, but a simple flux brush works fine. Remember glue swells the biscuits, so apply glue only to the parts to be joined, not the biscuits, and have clamps ready. Move quickly once they're inserted.

Flush Framing Joint

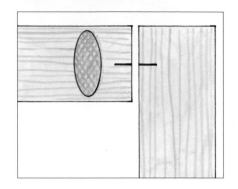

1 Cut the parts to length and place them in assembly position, then choose the largest biscuit that fits the stock and mark its center across the parts with a soft pencil.

Biscuited T Orientation

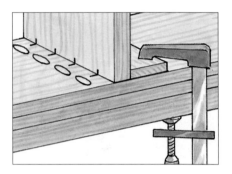

1 Clamp a guide across one part to line up the other in position so a row of biscuits can be laid out and marked on both parts.

Offset L Joint

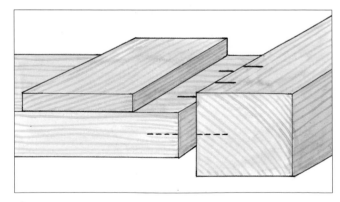

1 Mark for biscuits and stack a shim the same thickness as the offset on the thin part, using the stack to set the fence to cut at the thin stock's center.

2 Place the shim on the thin stock under the fence to cut mating kerfs at the index marks.

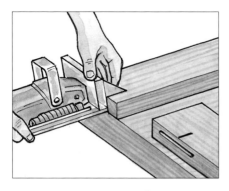

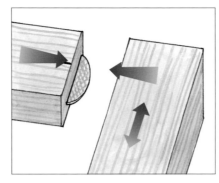

2 Adjust the 90-degree fence up or down to center the blade in the stock, set the machine for the biscuit size, index on the marks, and plunge in the blade.

3 Spread glue in the kerfs and surrounding wood but not on the biscuit, insert a biscuit and assemble the joint using the play in the kerfs to align the parts.

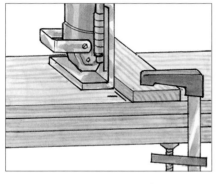

2 Set or remove the tool's fence so the nose is square to the base; align the base vertically against the straight guide and kerf to the marks, keeping within the joining part's outline.

3 Clamp down the second part and use the benchtop to reference the mating kerfs in the stock thickness at the index marks, then spread glue, insert biscuits, assemble, and clamp.

3 Without changing the blade height setting, kerf the thicker part at the index marks, then spread glue, assemble, and clamp as usual.

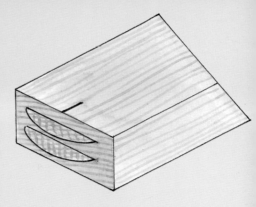

For extra strength or thick stock, use double biscuits by marking both sides of the wood and setting the fence to cut part way down the thickness from each side.

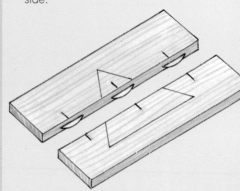

Very few biscuits are necessary to reinforce and align width joints; use the benchtop or 90-degree fence to reference the machine to the marks.

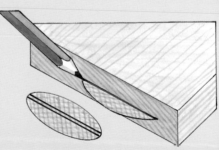

To fine-tune kerf depth, mark a biscuit, reverse it and re-mark; adjust the machine so the first line doesn't show when the biscuit is reinserted, and there is a small gap between the lines.

CHAPTER NINE

FASTENERS, HARDWARE, AND KNOCKDOWN JOINTS

There are occasions when temporary joinery is more convenient for large and restless pieces of furniture, or no joinery at all may be more suited to the purpose or status of the structure. Woodworking accommodates these contingencies with joints that disassemble and reassemble, and with old stand-by screws and fasteners, and modern inventions that work without glue or that reinforce glued joinery.

Using Wood Screws

Creating joints with screws isn't the common impression of woodworking, but screws make butted or lapped joints and reinforce or pin traditional joints. Screwed joints can be taken apart, and if assembled with glue, bond well without clamps.

The traditional woodworking screw with its flat, oval, or round head is being supplemented by hardened steel production screws. These screws have flat heads if designed for particle board or self-sinking "bugle" heads if they're designed for driving into softwoods, like drywall screws that have crossed over to woodworking from the building trades.

Steel screws are hardened for power driving with a drill/driver. They don't use the wood screw's typical slot drive. Instead they take advantage of the extra gripping power of Phillips, square, or combination drives. Sometimes they're coated so driving melts a heat-activated lubricant. Hardening makes screws brittle and, especially without a pilot hole, liable to break off in hardwoods. Soft brass wood screws have a similar problem that is remedied by pre-tapping the hole with a steel wood screw then replacing it with a brass wood screw.

Threads on wood screws climb around the screw at a lower angle than threads on hardened screws. The higher lead angle pulls hardened screws in quicker with fewer revolutions. The hardened screws' deeper threads, especially on particle board screws, create a tenacious grip that is less likely to strip out of the wood.

Besides the lustrous beauty of brass, bronze, or stainless steel over the hardened screw's dull blackened steel, wood screws often have the advantage of a bare shank section close to the head. This lets the screw spin in the wood anchor part and allows the threads to pull the front piece up tight against it. When threads are engaging both parts, any space between the parts won't close. The screw has to be backed out and the parts clamped together for joining.

Some production screws have auger points that will bore a pilot hole in softwoods, plywood, or particle board as the screw is driven. In hardwoods and dense sheet goods, the shanks and roots of both screw types require pilot holes and countersinking or counterboring for flat heads.

Screw Heads

The common wood screw is mild steel or brass and has one of three head types, either flat, oval, or round.

Bugle

Flat

Trim head

The three basic head styles of hardened steel screws are flat, bugle, or trim head for finishing work.

Screw Drives

The common types of screw drives and drivers in use are the straight slot, crossed Phillips, square Robertson drive, and a hybrid called combi, recex, or squarex.

Straight slot

Crossed Phillips

Square Robertson drive

Low profile pan heads, head washer and oversized washer heads bring a flat and increasingly large surface to bear on the wood.

Screws for Woodwork

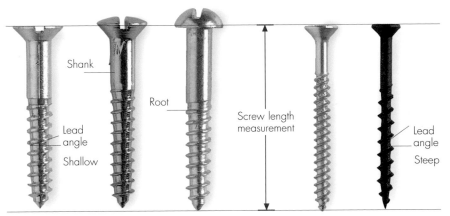

The different heads of wood screws sit flush or proud, the shanks are long and bare, threads climb the root at a low angle, and the root tapers to the tip.

Production screws sit flush or just below the wood surface, have a nearly straight profile, and double or single high-lead threads most of their length.

The confirmat is a firm-holding assembly screw for sheet good cabinets of plywood or particle board; it requires a pilot hole made by a special three-step drill bit.

To save time, some production screws have auger points or nibs under the head so that during driving the screw drills its own pilot hole or sinks itself into the wood.

Pilot Holes and Countersinks

The shank portion of the stepped wood screw pilot hole should extend through one piece so the threads will pull in the other piece and tighten the parts.

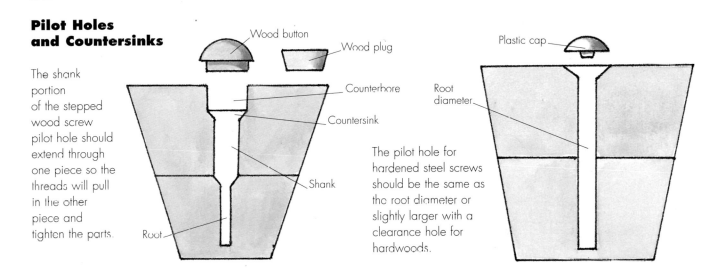

The pilot hole for hardened steel screws should be the same as the root diameter or slightly larger with a clearance hole for hardwoods.

A wood screw countersink can match a single screw size or adjust for a range of sizes with a tapered bit and moveable collars.

Moveable depth stop collar

Size 8 wood screw drill bit and countersink

When drilling for hinge hardware, Vix bits in three different sizes have a drill bit enclosed by a spring-loaded nose that helps to center the pilot hole.

Finishing washers in brass, black, or nickel plate hide the hole, increase the bearing area, and create a countersink for the screw head above the wood's surface.

Assembly Fasteners and Reinforcements

Using hardware to strengthen or hold furniture together is a technique as old as furniture itself. Today's hardware is more sophisticated and varied than the iron straps of old, and pound for pound is more effective. Mass production, built-ins, manmade materials, and the do-it-yourself market have inspired the development of special assembly hardware that is easy to install by manufacturers and consumers.

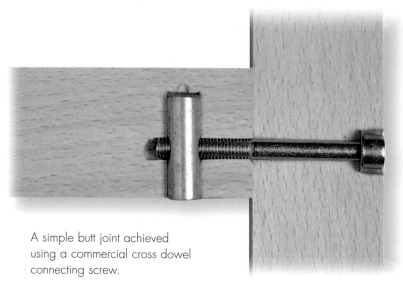

A simple butt joint achieved using a commercial cross dowel connecting screw.

Joining with assembly hardware is simple, often just by locating and drilling holes, inserting the mating hardware and adjusting it with a screwdriver or wrench. Plywood or laminated board cabinets butted together in "box" style construction sometimes use surface mounted or partially concealed connectors to join the parts, especially when they're sold unassembled as kits. Assembly hardware that permits easy assembly makes cabinets and long countertops easier to move in sections and join together on site. Certain assembly hardware, such as cross-dowels, adapts to reinforcing or creating hardwood furniture.

Not all projects warrant perfect craftsmanship. In the home shop, as in manufacturing, butted and hardware-joined construction eliminates time spent fitting joinery, gluing and clamping, and the associated tool requirements. The builder simply finds and installs hardware that holds parts in the required orientation. Hardware offers an alternative that saves time and money on projects that are not worth a large investment, like shelving and storage for the garage.

Threaded inserts are the biggest new thing to come in a small package. These cylindrical inserts come in several sizes of brass and steel with deep external wood threads that screw into a pilot hole and internal machine threads in common sizes. Inserts are an improved version of the old captured nut technique, which mortised a nut into wood, adding metal threads to grip assembly hardware like bedrail bolts. Although inserts have perimeter slots for driving, it's easier to thread them onto their special driving tool or onto a bolt against two "jam" nuts and drive them with a ratchet. Inserts add durable threads to wood for rigid assemblies or for jigs that are constantly being readjusted.

Width and Length Joints

Industry fasteners or "dog bones" were designed to join laminated countertops from the underside on site, but are useful for other length and width joinery, or in place of clamps.

Another product inspired by industry is knock-down or site assembly hardware designed to be epoxied into (center and right) or grip (left) biscuit joiner slots.

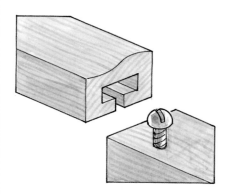

When inserted into a drilled hole, a special "keyhole" router bit cuts T-slotted keyholes (below) or routs a T-slot (above) to house round screw heads for joints that can be disassembled.

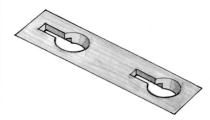

Surface-Mounted Hardware

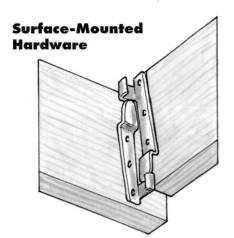

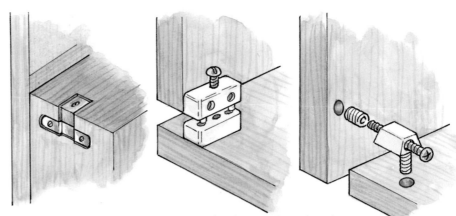

Plenty of serviceable but not particularly attractive interlocking hardware is available for most corner T or L joints.

Some joining hardware is based on the European cabinetmaking system of spacing a series of holes 32 millimeters on center or by surface mounting with screws to assemble the joints.

Partially Concealed Connectors

Many systems imitate the action of draw-bored mortises and tenons by catching the protruding head of a special screw in an eccentric nut *(Right)* that is tightened to pull the joint home.

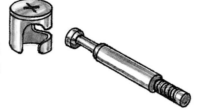

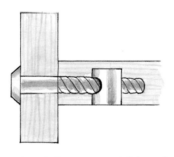

Cross dowels have a special threaded nut that is inserted into the part from below and adjusted so the screw threads engage the hole and pull the joint tight.

A relative of the cross dowel, the two-part connector bolt comes *(Above)* in two lengths and threads together from the insides of adjacent cabinets to anchor them.

"Locating dowels" use the 32 millimeter system of holes to thread into a part and line up with a mating housing nut that tightens over the dowel's head.

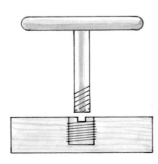

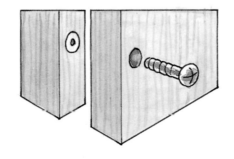

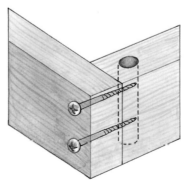

A T-tool or double-nutted bolt threads steel and brass inserts into wood to provide strong internal machine screw threads for joining.

Joints made by plain wood screws into a board's end will hold better if the fragile end grain is replaced by the better screw-holding power of a dowel's long grain.

Tabletop Fasteners

Store-bought or homemade tabletop buttons screw underneath the top, sliding in a groove in the apron with solid wood expansion, while the round desktop fastener is fine for plywood.

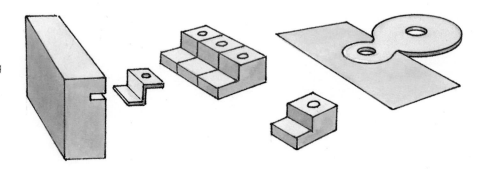

Cabinet Hangers

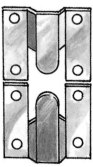

Light wall cabinets can be mounted with interlocking steel hardware or brass keyholes that fit over a screwhead to minimize wall damage; for heavier cabinets, use wood or metal hanging rails.

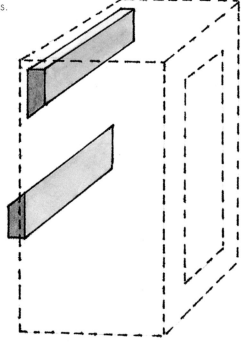

Bedrail Fasteners

For traditional work, a square-headed bedrail bolt with its nut mortised in from the bedrail's inside is covered with a metal cap to decorate and hide the access hole.

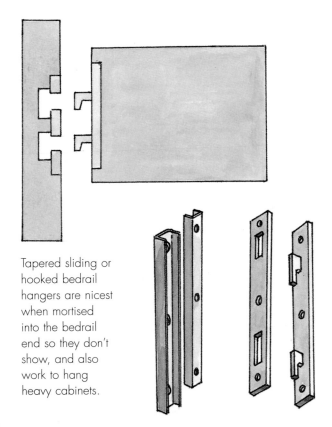

Tapered sliding or hooked bedrail hangers are nicest when mortised into the bedrail end so they don't show, and also work to hang heavy cabinets.

Corner Reinforcements

Plastic, steel, or brass reinforcements for every type of intersection are readily available in most hardware stores.

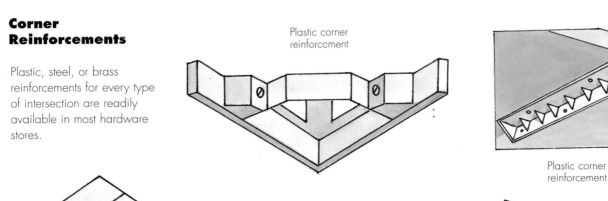

Plastic corner reinforcement

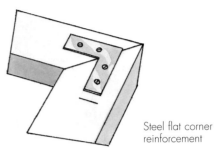

Plastic corner reinforcement

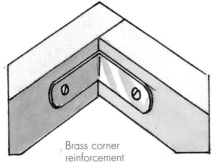

Brass corner reinforcement

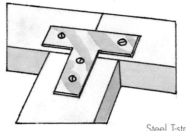

Steel T-strap reinforcement

Steel flat corner reinforcement

Wood glue block

Traditional wood reinforcing glue blocks can be made to fit any corner, but are best cut so the grain runs parallel to that of the reinforced parts.

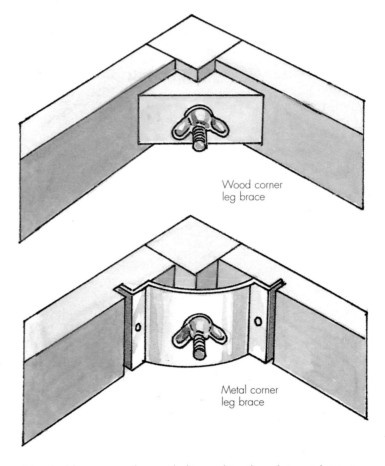

Wood corner leg brace

Metal corner leg brace

Use double nuts on a hanger bolt's machine threads to ratchet in its wood-threaded end, then tighten the wingnut onto a wood or metal corner leg brace.

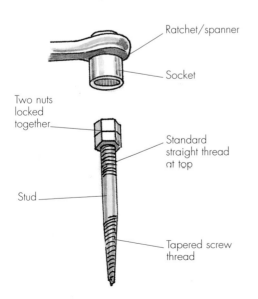

Ratchet/spanner

Socket

Two nuts locked together

Standard straight thread at top

Stud

Tapered screw thread

Wood Knockdown Joints

Furniture that breaks down into its components is part of a tradition that includes Roman military campaign furniture and "traveling" medieval trestle tables that were designed to be moved on a daily basis. The design of any large piece has to consider its bulk, weight, and maneuverability, if only to move it from the shop into the house. Woodworkers who enjoy the challenge of building all-wood structures that break down into smaller and lighter components will find the glueless knockdown joinery of old still useful today.

The through keyed or tusked tenon is a strong, visible joint that resists racking but has to be integrated with the overall design. A sliding dovetail mechanically interlocks to hold a structure invisibly, plus it breaks down and easily reassembles, especially when it's waxed. However, the effect of solid wood movement in the dovetail can't be compensated by tightening or loosening a tenon key, so sliding dovetails work best in short lengths or as a plywood tongue that stays stable.

The key mortises in tenons can be square or drilled round and use double wedged dowels inserted from each side as the key. After the tenon is scribed along its face to mark its exit, it's critical during layout that the key mortise be set back from this line. Otherwise the key won't bear on the upright to pull the joint tight, especially if the wood shrinks. The key mortise has to leave at least a finger's width of material in the short-grain section at the tenon's end or the grain will break out from the wedge's pressure on it. Sometimes the end of the key mortise is angled slightly to match the key.

To locate the attachment position of dovetail keys for fastening a table top, invert the leg and apron assembly on the underside of the top. Equalize measurements from opposite edges of the top to the aprons to center the assembly and outline the keys. In solid wood, the keyholes should be laid out across the grain so they won't restrain movement across the width of the top.

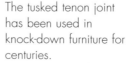

The tusked tenon joint has been used in knock-down furniture for centuries.

Keyed Tenon

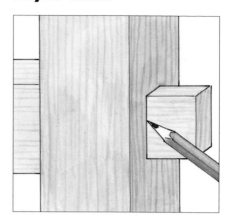

1 Make an overlong through tenon so it has some extending material that can be mortised, insert the tenon through, and mark its face where it exits its mortise.

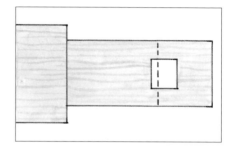

2 Lay out a mortise on the tenon, starting it just inside the line on the tenon face and leaving enough material to prevent short grain when the mortise is cut.

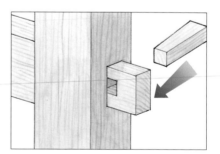

3 Make a key whose outside face tapers slightly and insert it through the mortise in the tenon so it bears against the upright and pulls the tenon tight.

Half-Dovetail Tenon

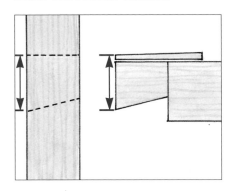

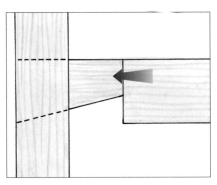

1 Lay out the through mortise for a half-dovetail tenon so its bottom end angles to the dovetail and the exiting side is long enough to include a wedge's thickness.

2 Make sure that the tenon can enter the mortise when its top edge is aligned with the top end of the mortise.

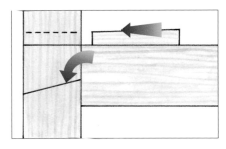

3 Insert the tenon and drop it down to fit the angles together, then slide in the tapered wedge, shaving it thinner until it stops flush with the tenon end.

Dovetail Key Top Fastener

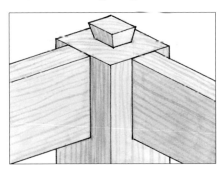

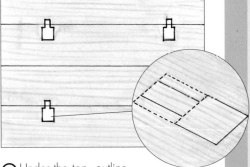

1 Cut a dovetail pin on each leg end so it will extend about ⅔ or ¾ into the thickness of the table top.

2 Under the top, outline the pin's widest end at the top's attachment position and scribe its neck width within the outline, marking an entrance hole to one side.

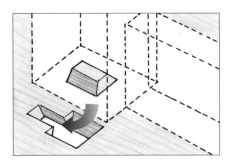

3 Consulting the related chapters, mortise a dovetail housing for the pin and an entrance hole to the right depth, insert the pin and slide it into the housing to lock.

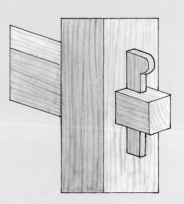

When rails are thick enough, tusk a tenon with a vertical wedge following the same procedure outlined for a keyed tenon.

To make moving or shipping easier, use unglued sliding dovetails to break bulky furniture into components, as in separating a desk into its modesty panel, end cabinets, and top.

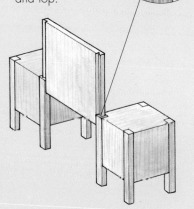

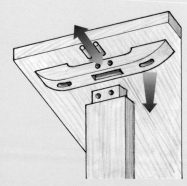

Removable pins in a blind tenon hold it tight but let the furniture be broken down for handling.

Glossary

Awl A pointed scribing tool used to mark layout lines. It works well with the grain, but has a tendency to fuzz up marks across the grain.

Beam The "handle" of a square or miter square as opposed to the blade, or the part of a marking gauge that holds the point.

Bending A tendency of wood to flex or the joint parts to pull away from each other under force on the side opposite an imaginary fulcrum.

Bevel A cut that is not 90 degrees to a board's face, or the facet left by such a cut.

Biscuit A thin, flat oval of compressed beech that is inserted between two pieces of wood into mating saw kerfs made by a biscuit or plate joining machine.

Bowing A lumber defect caused by drying. It makes the wood face bend up along its length like a rocker.

Box joint Another name for a *fingerlap* joint with straight, interlocking fingers.

Bridle joint A joint that combines features of both *lap joints* and *mortise* and *tenon*. It has a U-shaped mortise in the end of the board.

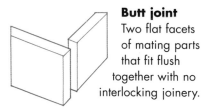

Butt joint Two flat facets of mating parts that fit flush together with no interlocking joinery.

Carcass The main body or frame of a piece of cabinet work.

Center lap A wide *dado* cut halfway into the thickness of a part to form half of a frame *lap joint*.

Check A crack in wood material caused by drying, either just in the surface or in the ends of the board so the fibers have separated.

Cheek The face of a *tenon, center lap*, or *end lap*, the long-grain walls of a mortise, or the long-grain mating surfaces of *dovetails* and their pins or *box joint* fingers.

Clamping blocks Blocks of wood that help distribute clamp force to the joint's gluing surfaces when correctly sized.

Combi drive A system for driving screws that incorporates more than one type of drive indentation in the screw head so it can be driven by several different drivers.

Combination square An all-metal, engineer-style square which can prove 90- and 45-degree angles. Its blade slides back and forth within the beam and can accommodate attachments like a centering head or a protractor.

Compound miter A cut where the blade path is not perpendicular to the wood's end or edge and the blade tilt is not 90 degrees to the face.

Compression Force on wood that pushes the fibers in on themselves, or a joint in on itself.

Confirmat An assembly screw for cabinets of manmade sheet goods.

Coping Sawing a negative profile in one piece to fit the positive profile of another, usually in molding.

Counterbore A straight-sided drilled hole that recesses a screw head below the wood surface so a wood plug can cover it, or the bit which makes this hole.

Countersink A cone-shaped drilled hole whose slope angle matches the underside of a flat screw head and sinks it flush with the wood surface, or the tool that makes this hole.

Crooking A lumber-drying defect which causes a lateral bend in a board.

Cupping A drying defect where one side of the board shrinks across the grain more than the other, causing the board to curl in on itself like a trough.

Cutting gauge A device which carries a small knife for deep scoring of layout lines parallel to an edge or for cutting veneer into strips.

Dado A flat-bottomed, U-shaped *milling* cut of varying widths and depths but always running across the grain.

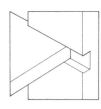

Dimensional conflict A situation where the long grain of the joined parts is glued or pinned perpendicularly and the natural fluctuation in the dimension of wood across the grain is restricted.

Double square A square which can prove 90-degree angles with its inside and outside corners and whose blade sometimes slides within a metal beam so it can be used as a depth gauge or marking gauge.

Dovetail joint A traditional joint characterized by interlocking fingers and pockets shaped like its name. It has exceptional resistance to tension.

Dowel pin A small cylinder of wood that is inserted and glued between two parts in mating holes to create or reinforce a joint.

Doweling jig Any of a number of commercially available devices to assist placing and drilling dowel holes. It can be shopmade.

Draw-boring A technique by which a joint is pulled home when a peg is hammered through it into slightly offset holes in the parts.

Dressing The process of turning rough lumber into a smooth board with flat, parallel faces and straight, parallel edges and whose edges are square to the face.

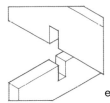

Edge lap A notch into the edge of a board halfway across its width that forms half of an edge lap joint.

Element A basic shaped part of a joint, either a *dado*, *rabbet*, *groove*, *pocket*, or square or angled cut, or combinations and modifications of these.

End grain The grain at the end of a board which can be likened to a bundle of straws cut across their length; it shows the tree's growth rings at various angles to the face of the board depending how the board was cut from the log. (See *flatsawn* and *quartersawn*.)

End lap A *rabbet* across a board's face at its end which forms half of a frame lap joint in an L or T orientation (not to be confused with an end-to-end lap, or *scarf joint*).

Engineer's square A precision metal square with a fixed blade for proving 90 degrees.

Face The widest part of the board as measured across the grain.

Fingerlap

A specific joint of the lap family which has straight interwoven fingers; also called a *box joint*.

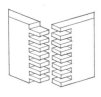

Flatsawn The most common cut of lumber where the growth rings run predominantly across the end of the board; or its characteristic *grain pattern*.

Grain pattern The visual appearance of the wood grain. Types of grain pattern include flat, straight, curly, quilted, rowed, mottled, crotch, cathedral, beeswing, or bird's-eye. For more on grain, consult a wood specialty book.

Groove A flat-bottomed, U-shaped *milling* cut whose depth and width can vary, but which always runs with the grain.

Half lap Another name for a *lap joint*.

Half pin In *dovetail joints*, the two outside pins of a row, named not because they are half the width of the others but because they are angled only on one side.

Halving In *lap joints*, a general term for a wide *rabbet* or *dado* cut halfway into the wood face or a notch cut in the edge; also another name for *lap joints*.

Hardwood Wood from broadleaf deciduous trees, no matter what the density (balsa is a hardwood).

Haunch

A secondary *shoulder* cut into the edge of a *tenon*.

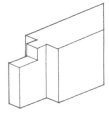

Housed

A situation where one part is enclosed fully or partially by another, or a specific family of joints.

Housing A *milled* cut, usually a *rabbet*, *dado*, or *groove*, but sometimes a *pocket*, which encloses all or part of a mating piece.

Index A reference *face*, mark or fence used to position a cut or bit, or the act of alignment.

Jig A shopmade or aftermarket device that assists in positioning and steadying the wood or tools.

Jointing The process of making a board face straight and flat or an edge straight, whether by hand or machine.

Kerf The visible path of subtracted wood left by a sawblade.

Key Not surprisingly, an inserted joint-locking device, usually made of wood.

Keyhole bit A special T-shaped router bit that cuts an extruded T path inside the wood thickness; the shape lets screw heads into the wood and the shanks slide along a groove that breaks the wood surface.

Knockdown joint

A joint which is assembled without glue and can be disassembled and re-assembled if necessary.

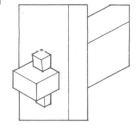

Lap   A type of cut, whether an *end lap, center lap,* or *edge lap,* used in *lap joints.* Also called a *halving.*

Lap joint
A type of joint made by removing half the thickness or width of the parts and lapping them over each other.

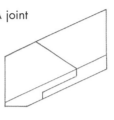

Length joint   A joint which makes one longer wood unit out of two shorter ones by joining them end to end.

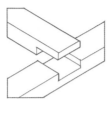

Lip   A glued-on or overhanging border of wood.

Long grain   The parallel fibers of the wood, like the length of a bundle of straws, that usually run parallel to the length of the board.

Marking gauge   An adjustable device with a steel pin or knife which marks a single layout line parallel to a wood edge.

Marking knife   Any knife, or a particular named style of knife, that is suitable for scribing layout lines.

Milling   The process of removing material to leave a desired positive or negative profile in the wood.

Miter   A generic term meaning mainly an angled cut across the face grain, or a specifically 45 degree cut across the *face, end grain,* or along the grain. See also *bevel.*

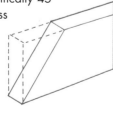

Miter gauge   A device that slides in a tabletop slot paralleling the blade of a tablesaw or bandsaw with a pivoting protractor head and fence to facilitate cross-cutting at different angles.

Mortise
The commonly rectangular or round pocket into which a mating *tenon* is inserted; mortises can be blind (stop inside the wood thickness), through, or open on one end.

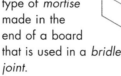

Mortise marking gauge   A device with two adjustable steel pins which mark two layout lines parallel to a wood edge.

Notch   A *dado* cut into the edge of wood that is part of an edge *lap joint* if it extends halfway into the wood width.

Open slot mortise   A type of *mortise* made in the end of a board that is used in a *bridle joint.*

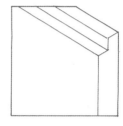

Orientation   The positional relationship between the parts in a joint—parallel, end to end or I, crossed, L, T, and angled.

Over-bearing   A type of router bit which carries the bearing above the cutter; a flush-trim over-bearing is particularly useful in template work because the template can be placed on top of the workpiece and the bit will cut the template's exact size.

Phillips drive   A method of engaging a screw head with its mated driver by a cross-shaped indentation in the screw head.

Pilot hole   A small drilled hole used as a guide and pressure relief for screw insertion, or to locate additional drilling work like *countersinking* and *counterboring.*

Pin   The part of a *dovetail joint* whose dovetail shape is

on the end of the board and fits between the tails; a screw or dowel used to reinforce a joint.

Plate joiner   A portable power tool dedicated to making slots or *kerfs* in the shape of an arc to fit *biscuits* in biscuit or plate joinery.

Pocket   Any hole or socket of various shapes which fit mated joint parts.

Quartersawn   A stable lumber cut where the growth rings on the board's end run more vertically across the end than horizontal and the grain on the face looks straight; also called straight-grained or riftsawn.

Rabbet
A milled cut which leaves a flat step parallel to, but recessed from, the wood's surface.

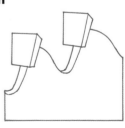

Racking   The tendency of a joint to loosen and change its angle, usually in relation to a structure which compensates with a change in the other joints, like a rectangle changing to a parallelogram.

Rail   The name of the horizontal parts of a door frame.

Raker tooth
A tooth type on some circular saw blades which is flat across its top so it can be used to make tolerably flat-bottomed grooves or waste material even by repeated passes across it.

Robertson drive   A Canadian screwdriving system that engages the screw by mating its driver to a square hole in the screw head.

Root The portion of a screw length below the head that has threads on it.

Scarf joint A joint that increases the overall length of wood by joining two pieces at their ends, commonly by gluing together unusually long *bevels* in their faces or edges.

Scribe To make layout lines or *index* marks using a knife or *awl*.

Shank The portion of a screw length below the head without threads on it.

Shear Force which pulls or pushes at a glueline or overloads a part to break it off.

Short grain Long grain whose fibers are cut across and left so short that the material becomes fragile and won't hold together.

Shoulder The perpendicular face of a step cut like a *rabbet* which bears against a mating joint part to stabilize the joint.

Sliding bevel A tool that has a changeable angle between its blade and beam. The blade length is also adjustable.

Slot drive A driving system for screws that mates the driver to a straight-grooved indentation across the head.

Slot mortise
A type of *mortise* made by machine bits that often has rounded ends (which can be squared).

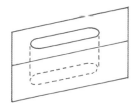

Softwood Wood from coniferous evergreen trees, no matter what the density (yew is a softwood).

Spline A flat, thin strip of wood that fits into mating grooves between two parts to reinforce the joint between them.

Split A situation where the wood material has broken along the grain. See also *check*.

Sprung joint An edge or width joint that has been planed slightly hollow to compensate for future moisture loss at the ends of the board which could shrink open the joint.

Step collar A wooden or metal device placed on a drill bit to gauge the hole depth.

Stile The name of the vertical parts of a door frame.

Story pole A layout stick that holds the actual-sized project in section view.

Straight grain The grain pattern that results when the wood is *quartersawn*.

Tail The part of a *dovetail joint* whose dovetail shape is cut into the face of a board and which fits around the *pins*.

Taper A cut with the grain which gradually angles along the board edge instead of running parallel to it.

Tenon The male part of a *mortise* and tenon joint, commonly rectangular or round, but not restricted to those shapes.

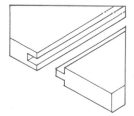

Tension Force on the joint or wood that pulls it in opposite directions.

Triangle marking A marking system that uses a simple triangle shape for marking wood to keep project parts sorted out.

Try miter A woodworker's testing device for 45-degree angles.

Try square A woodworker's testing device for 90-degree angles that sometimes follows specifications requiring only its inside corner to be square.

Twisting A drying defect in lumber that causes it to twist so the faces at each end of the board are in a different plane.

Wedge Usually a thin slice of wood that is glued into a *kerf* in the end of a through *tenon*; sometimes interchanges with *key*.

Whittling sticks Two straight, mated sticks that are placed on edge at opposite ends of a board and sighted across to prove the flatness of the lumber.

Width joint A joint which makes a unit of the parts by joining them edge to edge to increase the overall width of wood.

Wood movement The never-ending natural tendency of wood to expand and contract across the grain as its moisture content fluctuates in response to changes in relative humidity.

Index

Page numbers in *italics* refer to illustrations.

Quarto Publishing would like to thank Nicholas Pryke Productions for their permission to reproduce the picture on page 6 (left).

All other photographs are the copyright of Quarto Publishing plc.

We would also like to acknowledge and thank the following suppliers who kindly loaned tools and equipment featured in this book.

Axminster Power Tools
Chard Street
Axminster
Devon EX13 5DZ

Buck and Ryan
101 Tottenham Court Road
London W1P 0DY

Clico Tooling Ltd
Unit 7
Fell Road Industrial Estate
Sheffield S9 2AL

Colne Valley Fasteners Ltd
56 Wallingford Road
Uxbridge Road
Middlesex UB8 2RW

Franchi Locks and Tools
278 Holloway Road
London N7 6NE

G. Franchi and Sons Locksmiths
329–331 Gray's Inn Road
Kings Cross
London WC1X 8BZ

General Woodworking Supplies Ltd
76–80 Stoke Newington High Street
London N16 7PA

Joseph Marples Ltd
Clifton Works
John Street
Sheffield
S2 4QU

Parry Tyzack
329 Old Street
London EC1V 9LQ